Wanted
Words

Wanted
Words

From Amalgamots to Undercarments —
Language Gaps Found and Fixed

Edited by Jane Farrow

Foreword by John Ayto
Introduction by Michael Enright

Stoddart

Published in 2000 by Stoddart Publishing Co. Limited
895 Don Mills Road, 400-2 Park Centre, Toronto, Canada M3C 1W3
180 Varick Street, 9th Floor, New York, New York 10014

Distributed in Canada by General Distribution Services Ltd.
325 Humber College Blvd., Toronto, Ontario M9W 7C3
Tel. (416) 213-1919   Fax (416) 213-1917
Email cservice@genpub.com

Distributed in the United States by General Distribution Services Inc.
PMB 128, 4500 Witmer Industrial Estates, Niagara Falls, New York 14305-1386
Toll-free Tel.1-800-805-1083   Toll-free Fax 1-800-481-6207
Email gdsinc@genpub.com

04   03   02   01   00   4   5

Canadian Cataloguing in Publication Data
Main entry under title:
Wanted words: from amalgamots to undercarments —
language gaps found and fixed
ISBN 0-7737-6175-6
1. English language — New words — Humor. I. Farrow, Jane (Jane Katherine).
PN6231.W64W36 2000   428.1'02'07   C00-932088-1

U.S. Cataloging-in-Publication Data
(Library of Congress Standards)
Farrow, Jane.
Wanted words: from amalgamots to undercarments —
language gaps found and fixed /edited by Jane Farrow; 1st ed.
[144]p. : ill. ; cm.
ISBN 0-7737-6175-6
1. Literary recreations. 2. English language — Canada. I. Coburn, John, ill. II. Title.
402   21   2000   CIP

Cover design: Bill Douglas @ The Bang
Text design and typesetting: Kinetics Design & Illustration

As we put this book together, we tried our best to reach everyone whose ideas are
included. We ask your understanding if we were unable to contact you.

THE CANADA COUNCIL | LE CONSEIL DES ARTS
FOR THE ARTS | DU CANADA
SINCE 1957 | DEPUIS 1957

*We acknowledge for their financial support of our publishing program the Canada Council,
the Ontario Arts Council, and the Government of Canada through the Book Publishing
Industry Development Program (BPIDP).*

Printed and bound in Canada

Contents

Foreword

Think how the world has changed in the past hundred years — from flying machines to spacecraft, from wireless to computers, from cloche hats to bad hair days. It's not surprising that close on 100,000 new words have been added to the English language over that period. So many new things to talk about.

Where do all the words come from? Sometimes people actually sit down and try to invent them — in 1924, for instance, Henry Irving Dale and Kate L. Butler shared a prize of two hundred dollars for thinking up "scofflaw" to describe someone who disregards the law, and the word is still in use in U.S. English.

The vast undergrowth of specialized vocabulary, in fields as diverse as gas transportation and genomics, is kept in order by terminographers, who impose a necessary standardization. But, mostly, new words just bubble up of their own accord. To get their passport into the dictionary, they have to pass a range of tests relating to their frequency of use, the length of their currency, and the range of sources in which they have been found (to guard against individual writers plugging their own favourite neologisms!). The underlying idea is to ensure that a word has established a (relatively) permanent niche for itself in the language.

The one piece of equipment lexicographers lack is a reliable crystal ball (who would have dared predict ninety years ago that the word "radio" would win out over "wireless"?), so I shan't try to second-guess the English language over the fledgling words in this book.

But I wish them luck!

— John Ayto, editor of *Twentieth-Century Words,*
The Oxford Dictionary of Slang, and
The Oxford Essential Guide to the English Language

Wanted
Words

Introduction

There are really only two things you can do on the radio. You can play music, and you can talk. Use words.

Now, mind you, I once did an entire set of t'ai chi on live network radio. The reaction of the audience was intense indifference.

So it's words or music. And words are the paints that radio uses to create pictures in the mind. While many believe that only television is rich in visual imagery, in fact it is radio that creates indelible images in the imaginations of the listeners.

Over the past sixty or so years, the CBC Radio audience has come to expect that the people heard on CBC will use words correctly. After all, listeners own the damn thing, and they are merely being good bosses when they demand the best. Make a mistake and listeners will rise up in good-natured wrath. Use a word that sounds exotic or mysterious and the letters fly in. All of which shows that Canadians in general, and CBC Radio listeners in particular, love words. Word puzzles, crazy captions, silly neologisms, and dictionary quizzes of any kind — put those on the radio and audience response is guaranteed.

All of which brings me to Jane Farrow. Ms. Farrow is a *This Morning* producer with the energy of an Olympic sprinter and the imagination of Dr. Victor Frankenstein. Her story ideas are always unconventional and occasionally off the seismograph altogether.

During one story meeting in the fall of 1999, Jane came up with an idea for a game that involved making up new words to describe the mundane but hitherto unacknowledged elements of everyday life. We would spot the voids in the language and listeners would come up with their own terms to describe events or experiences that had so far gone unnoticed or unnamed by English-speakers

The response was overwhelming. Hundreds of clever and witty neologisms arrived within the first few weeks. We quickly set up a Web site and e-mail address to handle the weekly deluge of entries.

The Wanted Words challenge quickly became one of the most popular features on *This Morning*. Listeners submitted hundreds of new words each week. On three occasions, we received more than a thousand e-mails, faxes, and letters. Listeners were eager to play, and not just for the prize of a can of CBC promotional coffee.

People across Canada were having fun. Construction workers, farmers, bus drivers, academics, entire families, and grade-school classrooms all picked up on the challenge. Devoted Wanted Word players chatted and compared notes on our on-line discussion board. Listeners who made the short list basked in their moment of lexicographic glory. Others were miffed and slighted when someone in another part of the country won a prize for a word *they* had suggested.

We quickly drew up rules for determining which entry came in first, adjusting of course for regional time differences and the sluggish surface mail "co-efficient." Still, the West complained that the East was being favoured; Ontario alleged we were soft on Newfoundland. It became a hot item.

We soon realized that the Wanted Words challenge had the potential to reach beyond its radio audience (audioflation?). So Jane sat down and transformed the challenge into a book that will occupy you for hours.

As I read through it, I was struck by two things: first, the inventiveness of ordinary Canadians — inventiveness and imagination; and second, the undiminishing loyalty of listeners to CBC Radio.

So now it's your turn. Give these new words a whirl. You don't even need a radio.

— Michael Enright, host of *This Morning . . . The Sunday Edition*

About This Book

Let me tell you the story of Joy Strickland. She's an avid CBC listener, Wanted Words keener, and eighty-five-year-old dynamo, living out in Victoria, British Columbia. We called Joy up one day, so she could give us her latest word creation live on the air. She is the only person to whom we ever granted that privilege.

What compelled us to show her such favouritism? It was her dogged determination to contribute to the Wanted Words effort. You see, she had missed the previous week's deadline. She had tried to send her word by e-mail, but after she spent more than an hour waiting to use the public library's Internet computer, she went home and sent her entry via the slower but more dependable surface mail. Her dedication spoke volumes about the appeal this game has for many listeners.

What was Joy's motivation? A desire to hear her name on the radio? Maybe. A can of *This Morning*'s coveted coffee? Unlikely. The long answer would likely involve delving into some heady theories about the origins of language, semiotics, etymology, and ontology.

But let's leave that to the more pointy-headed among us.

I look at the game much more simply. When we play Wanted Words, we alleviate the familiar, low-level frustration we feel when we run into the gaps inherent in our language. Creating Wanted Words is, on some level, a refusal to accept these roadblocks. The originators of new words, such as Joy Strickland, don't just notice that English frequently fails us, they try to fix it.

The "wordies," as I like to call them, are the do-it-yourselfers of language building and semiotics. Where there's a will, there's a word. They are the stars of Wanted Words. On *This Morning* and in this book these little known legends of lexicography get their moment in the sun.

If you followed the Wanted Words game from its beginning back in October 1999, you'll know that we refined the rules a bit on the fly. Sometimes we'd lose sight of the original objective and pick entries that looked suspiciously more like phrases than words. We tried (unsuccessfully at times) to stay away from cheap puns, alliterations, and the scatological. Whenever we strayed too far, our listeners would let us know. What they wanted from Head Office, they told us, were clear rules and a level playing field.

We would also hear from them when they thought we picked the wrong word as the winner. And you know what? Sometimes they were right. On live radio, with the clock ticking towards the end of the hour, we occasionally made decisions we later regretted.

In this book, we've tried to right those wrongs. The words that head these chapters are not necessarily the same words that were chosen on-air. We did not always highlight the funniest or the cleverest words (although they are all there for you to enjoy). The words we chose are the ones we feel stand the best chance of eventually making their way into everyday use. Today, none of these words will make it past the spell-check on your computer. We hope that will change. Today, none of these words will make it past your opponent in Scrabble. We hope that will change one day, too.

Getting Wanted Words on the radio once a week involved a huge effort by a whole team of dedicated people. Every Thursday, I had the privilege of sitting across the table from two enormously talented hosts, who made my job so much easier. Michael Enright and I share a love of language and an admiration for the genius of our listeners. He taught me a lot about how to keep live radio "real" on the air, keeping me on my toes and pushing me to surprise him with some new twist each week. This made me nervous at first, but once I got the hang of it, I eagerly anticipated those moments when we would crack each other up with unscripted sniping and banter. The always generous Dick Gordon was also a treat to work with. He especially liked to play up our Wild West motif, describing, in considerable detail, my imaginary lime-green Naugahyde chaps.

My two Wanted Words "deputies," Lisa Ayuso and Max Paris, helped sort through the hundreds of e-mails, letters, and faxes every week. I also want to acknowledge the contributions of our first Wanted Words player Bill Casselman, our senior producer Peter Kavanagh, and the always inspiring Paul Wilson.

I owe an enormous thanks to Ira Basen, who was *This Morning*'s Executive Producer during the Wanted Words game, and my trusty editor. Each week I would spot a few voids in the language, draw up a short list, write the script, and head into his office for the fun-filled ritual bloodletting we call a "vet." He's an amazing writer and radio producer with a wonderfully dry sense of humour. He has an uncanny ability to foresee how it will all gel on the air, and now on the page. It was Ira who really pushed for this book, and without him it wouldn't have come together.

This book would never have happened without the support and help of Nelson Doucet and Don Bastian at Stoddart, editor Janice Weaver, and Barbara Brown and Bernie Lucht at the CBC. Research for this book was done by the multi-talented Erin Pettit at *This Morning*, and our smart and funny illustrations are by the wonderfully talented John Coburn, who has published three books of illustrations on New York City. All of these people worked extremely hard under an impossibly tight deadline, and managed to keep their wits and their senses of humour about them.

My fellow producers at *This Morning* are a constant source of support and smarts, and for that I am truly grateful. Finally, a heartfelt thank you to Sophie Hackett for being all-around amazing, all of the time.

As for the wordies, the entire English-speaking world thanks you for your brilliant new words — now let's all get out there and use them!

Jane Farrow

Amalgamot

Noun:

the combining of French and English words with similar
meanings to create a two-word phrase that means nothing.
Submitted by Brian Kelly

What can be more Canadian than this? This is the ripe fruit of decades of official bilingualism that requires packages and signs to carry words in both French and English. And when those words are placed side by side, as in "spout bec" on a carton of milk or "pont bridge" on a road sign, the result is an **amalgamot** — a rich, and often humorous, addition to our vocabulary.

Our listeners sent us a lot of examples, often accompanied by their own stories, including:

- **champignons mushrooms**
- **clous nails**
- **downtown centre-ville**
- **exit sortie**
- **femmes women**
- **free gratis**
- **grape raisin**
- **homard lobster**
- **jambon ham**
- **laine wool**
- **lune moon**
- **old fort cheese**
- **pamplemousse juice**
- **pont bridge**
- **riz rice**
- **spout bec**
- **stop arrêt**
- **stuffing farce**

K. Payne writes, "My father had a convenience store.
I remember as a kid how disgusted the American tourists
acted when they discovered that we had not only Orange
Crush, but also Raisin Crush."

Sharie Lomas of Vernon, British Columbia, says that her
family has been referring to their morning glass of citrus as
"pampel-moose juice" for years. "Our family has been calling
it this so long that our children have only just realized the rest
of the world calls it grapefruit juice. I wonder what strange
juice they thought they were drinking."

"The marquee for the Bytown movie theatre lists the day's
movies as 'Today Aujourd'hui.' A German post-doctoral
student at the National Research Council would pass by
the theatre on his way to the lab each day. After about two
months he remarked, 'My, that movie *Aujourd'hui* has been
playing a long time!'"

— *Linda Marchese, Ottawa*

"Hearing 'old fort cheese' referred to on the radio reminded
me of my old friend Ducki, from PEI, who used to feed her
cat tuna-thon catfood. It must have had tuna flavour that went
on and on for miles."

— *Jan Jorgenson*

"I used to work in a hardware store where a favourite
customer insisted on buying only 'clous nails' because,
according to him, their holding power in wood was far

superior to that of ordinary nails. To prove his point, he would point at the label, which read 'Clous Ardox Nails Hold Better,' and was clearly emblazoned by the Quebec-based manufacturer on all of its nail cartons."

— Jim Kitay, Midland, Ontario

And Julie Clark of Winnipeg wrote about her grandmother, who used to visit from England from time to time. Apparently she was fond of chicken, or at least of the way it was prepared for her here. "On a shopping trip to the local grocery story, she asked if we might buy another 'poul-ette chicken,' as she called it, because they tasted so much better than the regular chickens they had back in England."

Here's the short list of other words suggested by our listeners:

- **anglofrankenstein** — Sandra Waines, Huntsville, Ontario
- **bilabelism** — Sarah Salt, London, Ontario
- **bilingo** — Mike Madigan, Pasadena, Newfoundland
- **bimanglism** — Teresa Fowlie, Navan, Ontario
- **biminglism** — Teresa Fowlie, Navan, Ontario
- **bimingualism** — Dan Pernokis
- **canuckquialism** — Dolores Rintoul, Lake Audy, Manitoba
- **colanguinate** — Cameron Renwick, Huntsville, Ontario
- **duplexicon** — K. Christian, Tilden Lake, Ontario
- **englitch** — Kevin Whitlock, New Westminster, British Columbia
- **franglotango** — Paul McKinnon, Arnprior, Ontario
- **lingmingling** — Pat McCarthy, Halifax, Nova Scotia
- **manglicism** — Gary Disch, Aylmer, Quebec

- **mélanguage** — Jim Plaxton, Toronto
- **mot-word** — Jean-Louis Couturier
- **slanglais** — Doug Bowes, Victoria
- **synonom** — Gary Lovett, Winnipeg
- **trudeaulogism** — Jeff Parsons, St. John's

FYI

A note on franglais/frenglish: Both these words were suggested by many people, but they refer to an entire dialect

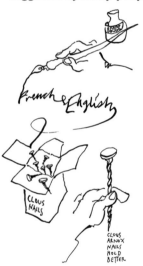

spoken across Canada. It is that curious blend of French and English that has language purists covering their ears and gnashing their teeth. *Je ne sais pas pourquoi,* because people *qui ne sont pas bilingue* have to *parlez avec* each other all the time — in *les places publique, les magasins,* subways and buses, *et surtout* in bars and restaurants. *Alors,* it's *meilleur* to be able to *communiquer un peu,* rather than to *communiquer rien, n'est ce pas?*

Aneurhythm

Noun:

the term for a song that sticks in your head, usually against your will.

Submitted by Rick Spanjer, Moose Jaw, Saskatchewan

Like a piece of gum stuck to your shoe, this is a tune that just won't leave you alone. It's there when you lay your head on the pillow at night, and it's there when you wake up in the morning. And worst of all, it's there all day. Sometimes the song itself may be good (I like Neil Diamond and ABBA), but at other times, it's a schlocky pop nugget that overstays its welcome (Barry Manilow's "Copacabana" or Whitney Houston's "I Will Always Love You"). But if it's there when you don't want it, it's an **aneurhythm**.

Here is what some other listeners called it:

- **adnausehum** — John Lichti, New Hamburg, Ontario
- **Barry Manilobotomy** — David and Gillian Calder, Vancouver
- **Billy-Ray virus** — Rob Morais and Diane Terry, Fredericton
- **eternatune** — Phyllis Jacklin, Walkerton, Ontario
- **glusic** — Sandi Forbes, Quesnel, British Columbia
- **humbug** — Ute and Thilo Joerger, Sackville, New Brunswick
- **humclinger** — Coleen Shepherd, Aylesford, Nova Scotia
- **hum-dinger** — John Pruner, Nepean, Ontario
- **humdumb** — Doug McLaughlin, Calgary
- **humnuts** — Leah Fisher, St. Albert, Alberta
- **humstuck** — Erica Prinn-McCarthy
- **inbrained melody** — John Bassett, Sudbury, Ontario
- **insongnia** — Brent and Lori Crichton, Waterloo, Ontario
- **malodee** — Graham Pilsworth, Halifax
- **melodhesive** — Anne-Gigi Chan, Coquitlam, British Columbia

- **melotinous** — Dick and Rita Timm, Vancouver
- **muse-ache** — Reba Terlson, Winnipeg
- **mustick** — Bev Leadbeater, Crystal City, Manitoba
- **obsessong** — Deidre Jewell, Galiano Island, British Columbia
- **songstruck** — Karna Trentman, London, Ontario
- **stuccato** — Irene Pramudito, Singapore
- **tunacy** — John Hawkins, Chezzetcook, Nova Scotia
- **tunami** — Drew Jacques and Mike Christos, Temagami, Ontario
- **tunebug** — Ute and Thilo Joerger, Sackville, New Brunswick
- **tunejam** — Linelle Lemoine MacDougall, Toronto
- **ubiquitune** — Faye Sherrard, Quispamsis, New Brunswick

FYI

It's hard to know what it is that makes a song into an aneurhythm. Scientists, psychologists, and ethnomusicologists have been studying the complex interplay of emotion, aesthetics, and musical sounds for centuries. They have discovered that certain sounds are naturally associated with certain emotions. For instance, a noise that rises rapidly in pitch is associated with happiness and joy. Low-pitched, droning noises connote grief. Anger is implied with sharp, percussive sounds that attack. Not exactly rocket science, is it? So why can't just anyone write a hit song? Even though the subtle emotional language in sounds and music can be annotated, it takes a songwriting ace to interpret it in new and appealing ways. But given the music industry's propensity for generic pop-rock, it does make you wonder if any producers have fed this formula into a computer and are handing out sheet music to their stable of hit paraders.

Here are some of the greatest aneurhythms of all time, as suggested by listeners (peek at your own risk):

- *Monday, Monday* — Mamas and Papas
- *Stayin' Alive* — Bee Gees
- *Snowbird* — Anne Murray
- *New York, New York* — Frank Sinatra
- *Pink Panther theme* — Henry Mancini
- *Maggie May* — Rod Stewart
- *Legs* — ZZ Topp
- *American Pie* — Don MacLean
- *Hey, Good Lookin'* — Hank Williams
- *Rhiannon* — Fleetwood Mac
- *Beethoven's Fifth Symphony*
- *Goldfinger* — Shirley Bassey
- *Gloria* — Laura Branigan
- *Takin' Care of Business* — Bachman Turner Overdrive
- *I Will Survive* — Gloria Gaynor
- *Feelings* — Morris Albert
- *A Hard Day's Night* — Beatles
- *Love Is a Battlefield* — Pat Benatar
- *Lady in Red* — Chris de Burgh
- *Coat of Many Colors* — Dolly Parton
- *Raindrops Keep Falling on My Head* — B. J. Thomas
- *Hotel California* — Eagles
- *Sweet Emotion* — Aerosmith
- *Both Sides Now* — Joni Mitchell

- ***Don't Worry, Be Happy*** — Bobby McFerrin
- ***Muskrat Love*** — Captain and Tenille
- ***All by Myself*** — Eric Carmen
- ***Holiday*** — Madonna
- ***The Unicorn Song*** — Irish Rovers
- ***anything by ABBA***

The best way to get rid of an aneurhythm is to force it out with another. Some listeners suggested the following "brain rinses," which are to be sung aloud until the original song gets unstuck.

- ***O Canada***
- ***Happy Birthday***
- ***Camptown Races***
- ***Kumbaya***
- ***Hockey Night in Canada theme***
- ***Iron Man*** — Black Sabbath

Bagmata

Noun:

the red lines that appear on the palm of
the hand as a result of carrying heavy plastic
grocery or shopping bags.

Submitted by Jennifer Chin, Windsor, Ontario

Gillian Calder of Vancouver spotted this void in the language. It is a by-product of the latter half of the twentieth century, when good old-fashioned paper bags gave way to plastic ones. This might have made carrying around wet heads of lettuce less risky, but we've ended up paying the price elsewhere — thousands of ragged plastic bags clinging to our highway ditches, hiking trails, and telephone wires. And those ugly red scars on the palm of the hand — ugh! This may not seem like the most pressing of gaps in our lexicon, but it did provoke some of the most creative responses. When we saw the word "**bagmata**," we were filled with admiration. Here's how Jennifer Chin explained where it came from:

"Dear Wizards of the Wanted Word,
I have some experience with this Wanted Word request. While I was working on my undergraduate degree in Toronto, I managed to wrangle myself a dream job at the downtown Eaton's empire: I was a mystery shopper. This job involved shopping in the various Eaton's departments for five to six hours at a time, evaluating the customer service of their sales associates. I quickly accumulated quite a few bags, which I then had to carry around the store. The weight of the bags would stretch the plastic handle into a thin, blade-like strip that would pierce my palms. At the end of the day, a mysterious, sore red line would appear in the palm of my hand. I eventually developed a callus across my palm as a result of the repeated and prolonged irritation. '**Bagmata**' is a word that I think aptly describes my experiences with this strange and menacing irritation."

— *Jennifer Chin, Windsor, Ontario*

Here are some of the other clever suggestions:

- **bagburn** — Judith Bushan, London, Ontario
- **bagcrag** — Hilary Ashby, Ottawa
- **bagony** — Valerie Roberts, Lakefield, Ontario
- **chafeways** — Andrea Wickham, Thetis Island, British Columbia
- **gripples** — Krista van Hiel, Glenburnie, Ontario
- **handle-mar** — Ron Hooper, Telkwa, British Columbia
- **handle-rips** — Phil Salem, Sioux Lookout, Ontario
- **holding patterns** — Sandra Waines, Huntsville, Ontario
- **load lesion** — Claire Budziak, Mississauga, Ontario
- **load lines** — Malcolm MacFayden, Victoria
- **lobclaws** — Charley Vaughan, Dartmouth, Nova Scotia
- **lug lines** — Susy MacGillivrary, Halifax
- **no-car-scar** — Kevin Bird, Ottawa
- **palm-a-grabbit** — Deb Cochrane, Kelowna, British Columbia
- **plastigmata** — Richard Facer, Noble, Ontario
- **president's chaff** — Margaret Hampshire, Terrace, British Columbia
- **rutabagga** — Ruth Janes, Toronto
- **sac-claw** — Steve Mosher, Toronto
- **sackcrack** — Terry Hall, Gander, Newfoundland
- **sactrack** — Gino Cormier, Miramichi, New Brunswick
- **schleplash** — Mary Barr, Toronto
- **shopmata** — Patti Gordon, Gore Bay, Ontario
- **shopper's lug-mark** — Harriet Mulder, Toronto

Cachablanca

Noun:

a place for safekeeping; valuables, once stored there,
are irretrievable because its location cannot be recalled.
Submitted by Raymond Gallant, Neguac, New Brunswick

It's hard to believe we still need a word for this fabled hiding spot — it has been swallowing our valuable keepsakes, tools, cash, and warranties for centuries. The appeal of this word is quite simple: we put these things in a secret cache, and then we blank when we go to find them. It's too bad we're not more like squirrels. The hippocampus of their brains somehow increases in size by 15 percent every autumn, which helps them keep track of the twenty-thousand-odd nuts they stash. Humans are pathetic in comparison. According to a recent study done in the U.K., we spend a year of our life looking for things we've misplaced in such clever places as the cookie tin or rubber boots.

Here are some other names for that elusive hiding place:

- **amnesium** — Nancy Fisher, Elora, Ontario
- **black hold** — Stephanie Chess, Guelph, Ontario
- **blockhole** — Bonnie Coukell, Gilbert Plains, Manitoba
- **deceptacle** — James MacEachern, Inverness, Nova Scotia
- **eludatriangle** — Bruce Hawn, Orillia, Ontario
- **elusafe** — Natasha Baronas, Prince George, British Columbia
- **fakekeeping** — Kathryn Anderson, London, Ontario
- **forgetfulnest** — David and Gillian Calder, Toronto
- **forget-me-spot** — Alan Major, Golden, British Columbia
- **forgrotto** — Paul Smith, Oshawa, Ontario
- **forsafen** — Susan Zagrodney, Williams Lake, British Columbia
- **hopeless chest** — Mike Gourgon, Belleville, Ontario
- **hyberspace** — Patricia Carter, Toronto

- **lost sock drawer** — Sam Lanfranco, Haliburton, Ontario
- **memory lox** — Thelma Wright, Broadview, Saskatchewan
- **miscache** — John Carter, Marathon, Ontario
- **mistachio** — Heather Pearson, Kingston, Ontario
- **Murphy's cupboard** — Sharon Moffat, Winnipeg
- **piggy blank** — Steen Petersen, Ottawa
- **squirrelheimer** — Linelle LeMoine MacDougall
- **treasure coffin** — Christine Moses
- **vaultzheimer** — Katya Androsoff, Calgary

Here are some listener tales from **Cachablanca**:

"This week's Wanted Word certainly strikes a chord with me. My husband has an overpowering feeling that some mysterious person is always trying to steal his binoculars. I have no idea where this notion originates, but because of it he always hides them away somewhere they can't be found — by anyone, including him. The longest time they remained 'safe' was about two years, which managed only to convince him further that they had been stolen. Eventually, I came across them by accident, in the box where the extra vacuum bags are kept. That also gives you a clue to how often I change those things.

"Anyway, I like to think of this 'safe' hiding place as the dun-gone, because when these things are hidden, they are as good as in the dungeon."

— *Norianne Kirkpatrick, Armstrong, British Columbia*

"I was listening to Wanted Words last night while hunting for my very own treasure coffin. I put away five hundred dollars in cash for the Y2K disaster, and I still can't find it. I could really use the money now!

"Anyway, my submission stands — treasure coffin."

— *Christine Moses*

"I am intimately acquainted with this place. It always seems terribly clever at the time. Presently, several things reside there: the dog's vaccination certificate, the beautiful Mother's Day card my son made me two years ago, and last year's perfect Christmas present for my aunt. These things are not lost or forgotten — they have been forsafen."

— *Susan Zagrodney, Williams Lake, British Columbia*

"After listening to Wanted Words, my wife, Elsie, and I exchanged a few ideas for this week's challenge that would reflect our experiences with putting things away in a safe place and then not remembering where it was. We thought we had a couple of sure winners, but we decided to 'put them away in the back of our minds' until later. Though not usually prone to memory lapses, we were taken aback just a bit when within a few hours we couldn't remember either the expressions we had coined or the actual Wanted Word you were seeking. Fortunately, I was able to click onto your Web site today and decided to send these suggestions before lapse #2 sets in.

"A few years ago, just as my wife and I were leaving on a much-needed winter holiday, my father-in-law gave me a hundred-dollar bill as a going-away gift. However, because our holiday destination didn't give a very good exchange on Canadian money, I decided to leave it at home, in a safe place. I put the money (or so I thought) in the breast pocket of one of my suit jackets (older, tight-fitting suits) at the back of the clothes closet. I remember my late father-in-law telling me to 'put it somewhere that is easy to remember but difficult for anyone else to find.' That was at least ten years ago, and I still haven't found it. (Maybe I gave the suit with the hundred dollars in it to a used-clothing collection agency, but I don't remember.)

"One of the words we use for this place is the forget-me-not spot."

— *Floyd and Elsie Williston*

"Here's a tip for improving the odds of finding something after you've deposited it in your vaultzheimer: Stop looking for it. Look for something else instead. When you are looking for something you want, you almost never find it, but you almost always find something else that you were looking for before and probably no longer need."

— *Katya Androsoff, Calgary*

Chillbrain

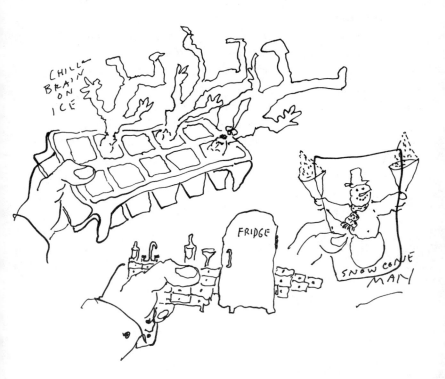

Noun:

a term for the headache caused by drinking or eating
something very cold.

Submitted by Irene Rogers, Salmon Arm, British Columbia

Chillbrain

This word was requested by Bill Plewes of Fraserville, Ontario. Scientists commonly refer to it as the "ice cream headache," but we knew our listeners could do better than that — and they did. There were many fine entries. We liked **chillbrain** not only because it describes the phenomenon very well, but also because it can be used in conjunction with the word "chilblain," which is the painful swelling of your fingers, toes, or ears when they are exposed to cold.

Some people don't get chillbrains, but for those who do the pain is very real. It derives from a numbing of the skull caused by the constriction of blood vessels in the back of the mouth and the palate. This transports pain along some vital blood vessels to the back of the eyes and forehead. The sensation lasts about a minute, and the temperature of your forehead actually drops slightly. The only way to avoid a **chillbrain** is to suck on those ice cubes and snow cones slowly.

Here are some of the other suggestions we received from listeners:

- **arctic forehead** — Michael Ennis, Salmon Arm, British Columbia
- **brainsicle** — Maurice Hoag, Winnipeg
- **burrrsitis** — Doug Millman, Burk's Falls, Ontario
- **chilly-wack** — Patricia Carter, Toronto
- **coldfront** — Greg Evans, Vancouver
- **cryocranium** — Shayna Kravetz, Toronto
- **eskimo piegrain** — Jane Keelor, Colborne, Ontario
- **facia glacia** — Bob Thornton, Richmond, British Columbia

- **freezer-seizure** — Suzette Delmage and Chris Hutchence, Whitehorse, Yukon
- **freizure** — Raymond Leduc, Bromont, Quebec
- **fridgehead** — Tracey Rein, Chilliwack, British Columbia
- **frigid-hair** — Kee Mushenheim, Gaspereau, Nova Scotia
- **icegrain** — Greg Leibert, Antarctica
- **numb-skull** — Drew Hegadoren, Kamloops, British Columbia
- **pangfroid** — Bill McGibbon, Halifax
- **slush-rush** — Dave Owens, Fredericton
- **toboggan noggin** — Robin Bergart, Toronto

Cranksinatra

Noun:

the sound an engine makes when it is trying to start;
most commonly heard on cold winter mornings.

Submitted by Anonymous

Just as the cry of the loon defines the Canadian summer, the sound of a desperate attempt to coax some life into a stone cold engine permeates the Canadian winter landscape. This often futile search for internal combustion frequently begins with a prayer, followed by several expletives strung together. More often than not, it concludes with a call to the motor league.

We thought the word "**Cranksinatra**" described this phenomenon quite well. "Sinatra" suggests the song you hope your engine will make, while "crank" harks back to an earlier era when, for all we know, cars were easier to start. It also doesn't hurt that the whole ordeal often leaves the driver feeling kind of cranky.

Here are some other possible words:

- **arctic-choke** — Barry Van Dusen, Amherstview, Ontario
- **assaultonbattery** — Glen Leinweber
- **booster-crow** — Kelly Sali, Kelowna, British Columbia
- **car-rumba** — Doug Millman, Burk's Falls, Ontario
- **cargling** — Les Deacon-Rogers, Stewart, British Columbia
- **chokemon** — Mary and Paul Monteith, Kitchener, Ontario
- **coldcrank** — Corrado Mallia, Calgary
- **combusted** — Ryan Scranton, Carleton Place, Ontario
- **crangst** — Colin MacDonald, Barrie, Ontario
- **crank-call** — Vern Yoshida, Nanaimo, British Columbia
- **cranktankerous** — Bob, Sidney, British Columbia
- **engina** — Judy Delogne, Calgary
- **enginausea** — Chris Hutchence and Suzette Delmage, Whitehorse, Yukon

- **frignition** — Angus Ferguson, Meacham, Saskatchewan
- **hesignition** — Jim Coady
- **ice whine** — Lou McIntyre, Rothesay, New Brunswick
- **stagnition** — Neil Slater, Regina
- **startering** — Kenn Doerksen, Winnipeg
- **wreckignition** — Hap Wilson, Port Carling, Ontario

FYI

"My car wouldn't start" is wearing a bit thin as a standard excuse for skipping work. The Mother of All Excuses Place is a Web site that has catalogued thousands of excuses for being late or absent for just about anything. Try out some of these zingers on your boss:

- "I spent my paycheque on lottery tickets, and I'm out of gas till payday."
- "I left rubber cement next to my bed while I was sleeping and got really high. When I woke up, I fell on a flashlight butt-first."
- "My car tires got stuck in the streetcar tracks! I could drive forwards and backwards, but I couldn't turn off the tracks. I had to drive all the way down to the rail yards to get free."

- "I tried to dye my hair blonde, but it came out green!"
- "Someone smashed in my windows this morning with a large, blunt object."
- "We're trying for a baby and the doc says the next few days are our best chance."
- "Sorry, I can't make it in to work today. I have amnesia. I'm not even sure if I work there."
- "My cat is lonely and stressed out, and if I don't spend quality time with him, he will keep peeing on the furniture."
- And, since some people still consider homosexuality a sickness, they could use it as an excuse to skip work: "Sorry, I can't come in to work today. I'm gay."

Double Os

Noun:

the word voted most likely to be used to
refer to the decade between 2000–2009.

Submitted by Steven Goodman, Winnipeg

Although baptizing an era before it happens is difficult, if not impossible, anyone who came up with a simple, all-purpose moniker for the next decade was pretty much assured beers for life, courtesy of the lexicography hall of fame. For months leading up to January 1, 2000, lexicographers pondered this tantalizing gap in the language and columnists begged readers to suggest some possibilities. Various contests encouraged folks to vote for their favourites — in the U.S., the two-kays was favoured, while the Brits picked the zeros. CBC listeners did not disappoint, devising a bevy of whip-smart suggestions that we posted on our Web site in December. Fifteen hundred people cast their ballots, and here are the results:

1. the double 0s — Steven Goodman, Winnipeg *(31 percent)*
2. the naughties — Jennifer Russell, St. John's *(21 percent)*
3. the two-kays — Atul Kapur *(15 percent)*
4. the zips — Kathy Ehman, Strathcona,
   Prince Edward Island *(7 percent)*
5. the naughts — Philip and Marie Garrison, St-Polycarpe,
   Quebec *(5 percent)*

These other suggestions trailed far behind, in the following order:

6. the oonies — Andre MacNeil, Iqualuit, Nunavut
7. the pre-teens — Jeff Poss, Waterloo, Ontario
8. the aughts — The Garrys, Oak Harbour, Washington
9. the doozies — Hank Dayton, Waterloo, Ontario

10. **the millies** — Paula Strasberg, Toronto
11. **the zeros** — Tim Storey, Cormac, Ontario
12. **the primes** — Ken Bauman
13. **the singles** — Douglas Ford, Kingston, Ontario
14. **the millicents** — Doug Millman, Burk's Falls, Ontario

FYI

Babies born between 2000 and 2009 may have to live with the stigma of phrases like these:

- *"I am a child of the silly nillies."*
- *"I'm a naughty aughties baby."*
- *"I was born a swinger of the singles."*

Flufe

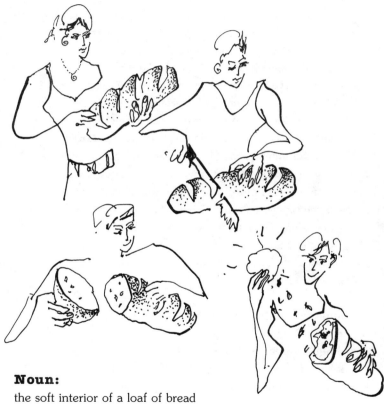

Noun:
the soft interior of a loaf of bread
(i.e., not the crust).
*Submitted by Michael Armstrong,
Prince George, British Columbia*

• • • • • • • • • • • • • • • • • • • •

A colleague of Jacqueline Wallis's spotted this void in the language while getting her hair done and chatting with some French women in the salon. They could barely believe that English-speakers didn't have a word for the middle part of a loaf of bread. Being consummate bread lovers, the French call it *la mie*. But why **flufe**? Well, we're not entirely sure, but we certainly like its fluffiness. **Flufe** just rolls off your tongue, airy and chewy all at once. Like the words "whack" and "tuba," **flufe** somehow sounds like the thing it describes.

This Wanted Word challenge was not without its controversy. According to some of our listeners, there is already a perfectly serviceable English word for **flufe**. "Crust or crumb?" is the phrase people use when asking a guest what sort of bread slice he prefers, the chewy interior or the crusty heel of the loaf. Some will undoubtedly prefer to revive the old word "crumb," but others insist it should be put out to pasture, since it clearly does double duty in the deeply meaningful world of bread.

For the trailblazers among us, here's a list of other wonderful suggestions:

- **anti-crust** — Margaret Hampshire, Terrace, British Columbia
- **dough-nugget** — Joy Strickland, Victoria
- **inbread** — Mal Cohen, Dartmouth, Nova Scotia
- **interloaf** — Charlene Boyce Young, Halifax
- **leaven-heaven** — Betty Ford, Innerkip, Ontario
- **leavenworth** — Andrew Tutty, Georgetown, Ontario
- **loafmeat** — Carl Heineken, Montreal

- **midough** — Terry MacIntosh, Guelph, Ontario
- **purebread** — Toni Lyons-Mindzak, Ottawa
- **softcore** — Dale Bemben, Gloucester, Ontario
- **spread-bed** — Randy Holte, Penticton, British Columbia
- **wheatmeat** — Andrea Wickham, Thetis Island, British Columbia

FYI

Impress your friends and co-workers with these bread-related vocabulary builders:

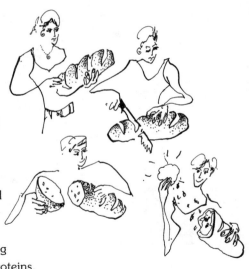

- **break and shred**: the rupture that occurs along the top of a loaf's round upper crust when it is baked. Sometimes described as "wild."
- **bloom**: the colour of the crust. It is the result of heat-induced carmelization of sugars and browning reactions involving carbohydrates and proteins.
- **occluded air**: the bubbles or voids in the inside of a loaf. This is created by mixing the dough or batter, and by yeast or chemical leavening.

Forevuary

Noun:

the long, cold, dark span between New Year's Day
and Good Friday.

Submitted by Brian Carty, Fredericton

There are many joys associated with living in Canada, but **Forevuary** is not one of them. In most provinces, there are no statutory holidays between January 1 and the Easter weekend. That means we have to endure the darkest, coldest, bleakest time of the year without even the promise of a long weekend to sustain us. Some years, when Easter comes late in April, **Forevuary** can last more than a hundred days. And each and every one of those days can feel like forever. Here's a short list of other names for this interminable stretch:

- **bleakstreak** — Suzanne Langdon, Kitchener, Ontario
- **bunny-stretch** — Sylvia Legris, Saskatchewan
- **coldrums** — Mary Ann Westad, La Glace, Alberta
- **the Dark Ages** — Adrian Telizyn, Fort St. John, British Columbia
- **daylight-waiting time** — John L. Hill, Toronto
- **draguary** — Michael Evans, Regina
- **hiberlude** — Jim McPherson, Milford, Ontario
- **holidearth** — Ed Belzer, Shubenacadie, Nova Scotia
- **invernal** — Brian Lloyd, Saskatoon
- **preaster** — Sandra Waines, Huntsville, Ontario
- **spring bleak** — Bob Orr, Saltsprings, Nova Scotia
- **sprinter** — Robert Gervais, Greenfield Park, Quebec
- **winter slowstice** — Karna Trentman, London, Ontario
- **winterminable** — P. A. McKenzie, Toronto
- **wintermission** — Valerie Broman, Kelowna, British Columbia
- **winterned** — John Perry, Vancouver
- **winterval** — Trish Gorie, Nepean, Ontario

FYI

Fact: Easter is the first Sunday following the full moon that comes after the vernal equinox.

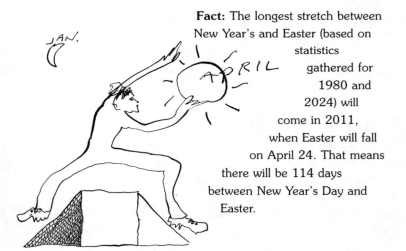

Fact: The longest stretch between New Year's and Easter (based on statistics gathered for 1980 and 2024) will come in 2011, when Easter will fall on April 24. That means there will be 114 days between New Year's Day and Easter.

Gournot

Noun:

a person who really wants to be able to cook, but just
can't seem to get anything right. The opposite of a gourmet.
Submitted by Beth Charette

Gail Norcross asked us to find this word. Think of this person as the anti-Martha. Just as Ms. Stewart can do no wrong in the kitchen, a **gournot** can do no right. If you are invited to Martha's house for dinner, you'll probably not want to eat for a day or two before the event. If you are heading for a meal at the home of a **gournot**, however, you may want to grab a burger on the way over because you already know two things: the meal will be late, and it won't be worth the wait. **Gournots** shouldn't be confused with junk-food junkies, however. Unlike these fans of processed and frozen foods, **gournots** often love eating gourmet food — they're just dyspatular in the extreme. And the sad part is that it won't be for lack of trying. You can picture a **gournot** watching Martha's show, reading her mags, taking notes, hoping to find the secret that will break the curse. But alas, there is every indication that this is a lifetime affliction.

Here are some other great suggestions from our listeners:

- **cheflexic** — Dino Giurissevich, Penticton, British Columbia
- **cordon blah** — Jim O'Rourke
- **culinscary** — Leslie Balsillie, Harrow, Ontario

- **dyspatular** — Richard Scott, Grimsby, Ontario
- **epicurse** — Lorne Wald, Montreal
- **garrotting gourmet** — Bob Halliday, North Bay, Ontario
- **gastronaut** — Bavarian Wine Works Wenches, Kimberley, British Columbia
- **gourmain't** — Chris Lambie, Halifax
- **grub dependent** — Brian Genn, Pender Island, British Columbia
- **inepicurean** — Tony Rideout, Lethbridge, Alberta
- **Martha Screwup** — Phyllis Jacklin, Toronto
- **meal-mangler** — Judie Marsden, Stittsville, Ontario
- **non-vivant** — Jim Chliboyko, British Columbia
- **no-pan-doo** — Lynnie McLellan, Waterloo, Ontario
- **shlepicure** — Scott Piatkowski, Waterloo, Ontario
- **skillettante** — John Shepherd, Toronto
- **water-burner** — Bob McLarty, Ottawa

Here's a little recipe for Gournot Delight, submitted by Valerie Broman of Kelowna: "Back in his college days, my husband had a roommate who was an inepicurean. He lived in fear of G.'s turn at cooking. One night, G. made pizza. To David's surprise and disgust, the pizza consisted of white bread spread with ketchup and topped with cheddar cheese and ground oregano. He broiled it in the toaster oven."

Grog Fog

Noun:

the fuzzy-headed stupor associated with a bad hangover.

Submitted by Ian Ross, Calgary

Hangovers are complex medical conditions that seem to affect some drinkers more than others. But for those predisposed to drinking large volumes of peppermint schnapps, American beer, and homemade red wine and topping that off with MSG-laced Chinese food, **grog fog** is a familiar enemy.

Grog fog is intellectually crippling. Unable to formulate thoughts coherently or remember names, those afflicted try counting aspirins and relearning basic language skills. Sound it out slowly — grrrrooggg ffffoooogggg. That's very good. Now lie down somewhere quiet and savour the rest of these listener suggestions:

- **alcophasia** — John Rudzinski, Hull, Quebec
- **boozeflu** — Pat Pitcher
- **brunk** — Heather Dootoff, Saskatoon
- **buzz fuzz** — Vera Jenkins
- **cereblur** — Doug Speers, Summerland, British Columbia
- **delibatated** — Ron Stoltz
- **flannelous** — Brian Wojtowicz, St. Mary's, Prince Edward Island
- **fluzz** — Patty Roy, Kakabeka Falls, Ontario
- **frontal lebottleme** — Ross Jarvis, Toronto
- **jughead** — David Whiteley
- **mentalpause** — Lisa McBurnie, Truro, Nova Scotia
- **neurofizzle** — Michael Zigler, Toronto
- **perpluted** — Kirk Hughes
- **raisinbrain** — Phil Scott, Plattsville, Ontario
- **rum-skull** — Brent Daignault, Calgary

Grog Fog

- **the stupies** — John Knops, Yukon
- **Teflon head** — Jasmine Qureshi, Olds College, Alberta
- **thumphead** — Adrian Cooper, Kingston, Ontario
- **twenty-four-ounce flu** — Kay Griffiths, White Rock, British Columbia

FYI

Canadians are a nation of beer drinkers, but unlike some guy called Joe, we're not all patriotic. For five years running, imported beer sales have taken a bite out of the market share of domestic beer. But who are we fooling? Even in their worst year, domestic brands still accounted for 93 percent of the beer market. Big whoop for the leftover 7 percent — that's about one Corona a year for most people.

Wine's a different story. Well over half the rotten grape juice we drink is imported, and a lot more of it is red in colour than used to be the case. Back in the 1980s, we couldn't slosh back enough white wine spritzers. Ten years later, red wine has almost doubled in popularity and is only a few points away from the halfway mark in national consumption trends. Only Quebecers have figured out that red wine tastes better, and that's why they sip on it 64.7 percent of the time.

But cooler consumption is the hottest trend in the drinkin' business. People can't get enough of these pre-mixed, syrupy, fizzy alcohol drinks. There must be an underground syndicate of thirteen-year-olds buying them — who else would drink goo-goo berry vodka parfait?

Hameo

Noun:

the bit part played by people who try to get on
television by standing, waving, or jumping up and down
behind television news reporters or sportscasters.

Submitted by Chris Lawson, Winnipeg

Hameo

John Wroe of Haileybury, Ontario, alerted us to this amusing gap in the language. Like a moth to the flame, the tele-bitionist is drawn to the bright sun-guns atop the TV cameras. Caught in the crosshairs of millions of viewers and millions of dollars of production money, the kamera-kaze has crucial information to deliver — party on, dude! Perhaps he can't afford stamps and needs to get the "hi, Mom" message out somehow. Whatever motivates these hop-arazzi, they drive people in the TV business to distraction. Here's a letter from someone who is growing weary of **hameos**:

"I was a television producer in Winnipeg for many years, and these individuals are all too familiar to me. They are attracted by cameras and think that we all are to be rewarded by their appearance on our screens. This rises to the height of lunacy when they see themselves on the monitor and begin making faces akin to those of a child discovering a mirror for the first time. Canadians who stayed awake on New Year's Eve 2000 to catch the first live hit from celebrations in Kelowna were rewarded with on-screen pandemonium as these people scrambled to get their faces on camera, almost taking over the airwaves. And last summer at the opening ceremonies for the Pan Am Games, the supposed VIPs behind Princess Anne made faces and threw popcorn at each other. My suggested word for these people is 'telegoons.'"

— *John Prentice, Winnipeg*

Here are some other clever listener suggestions:

- **backgroundhog** — Elfriede Budgey, Truro, Nova Scotia
- **cameroddity** — Marion Haffner, Winnipeg
- **cam-ham** — Ron Barnett, Flesherton, Ontario
- **collateral-hammage** — Greg Lainsbury
- **hi-mombicile** — Rex Trailore, Manitoulin Island, Ontario
- **hop-arazzi** — D'Arcy Mackay
- **jerk-on-the-box** — Tracey, Chilliwack, British Columbia
- **kamera-kaze** — Jackie Lochhaas-Gerlach, Kingston, Ontario
- **newscrasher** — Brenda Gluska, Toronto
- **newsmonkey** — Kimberley Smith, Vancouver
- **on-airhead** — Louis Gravel, Victoria
- **parasight** — Lenny DeSchutter, Rapid City, Manitoba
- **tele-bitionist** — Marion MacLeod, Halifax
- **telegoon** — John Prentice, Winnipeg
- **teletwirp** — W. Bell-Stewart, Nanaimo, British Columbia
- **teleweasel** — Enrico Carlson Cumbo, Toronto
- **videhographer** — Grant Fines, Peterborough, Ontario
- **vidiot** — Jim Connors, Dartmouth, Nova Scotia
- **warhollering** — Christopher Wells, Hunter River, Prince Edward Island

Herbicidal Maniac

Noun:

a person who kills plants; the opposite of a green thumb.

Submitted by Jeff Daniels, Kitakami-shi, Japan

Talin Vartainian of Toronto suggested this challenge, and in retrospect, it's hard to believe we've functioned this long without this killer word. Listeners quickly filled this gaping hole in the English language with a florid array of suggestions that filled us with awe. **Herbicidal maniacs** walk among us, but you'd never know one to see one. They prey on healthy plants and shrubs, smuggling them home in bags and boxes, then slowly finishing them off with climate-controlled torture. Herbinators don't mean to be monstrous. Most of their innocent victims are killed with kindness, the unfortunate recipients of too much water or too little sunlight.

Here's the short list of other listener suggestions:

- **bloominator** — Mark Trigg, Nepean, Ontario
- **botanicidal** — Kimberley Juras, Harrow, Ontario
- **botchanist** — Kelli Leaujay, Winnipeg
- **darth vegan** — Bruce Bauman, Cumberland, British Columbia
- **the de-germinator** — Darlene Boudreau, Beresford, New Brunswick
- **earth-smother** — Paddy Muir, Halifax
- **fleurderer** — Judith Bond and Ken Albanese, Fergus, Ontario
- **fleurfatale** — Jean Lewis, Ottawa
- **floraputz** — W. Bell Stuart
- **flortician** — Marie Weeren, Halifax
- **gangrene thumb** — Evelyn Henke, Chipman, Alberta
- **grass-assin** — Victor Wong, Ottawa
- **green-reaper** — Jean-Louis Couturier, Montreal

- **grim keeper** — Lynn Comish, Paradise, Nova Scotia
- **growth negligence** — Carolyn DeCoster, Winnipeg
- **herbinator** — Janice and Robert Castel, Courtenay, British Columbia
- **hortician** — Glenda Rathwell, Victoria
- **horticidal maniac** — Lucille Carter, Alexandra, Prince Edward Island
- **hortikillturist** — Nancy Holland, Halifax
- **involuntary plantslaughter** — Veronica Morley Hubert
- **mean thumb** — Henry Gauthier, Montreal
- **morticulturist** — April Sampson, Weyburn, Saskatchewan
- **mouldfinger** — Ric Doedens, Toronto
- **necrofloriac** — Bill McKibbon, Halifax
- **numb thumb** — Rick Callahan, St. John's
- **plantagonizer** — Sioban Mullin
- **planter's thwart** — Phil Barbeau, Sudbury, Ontario
- **roto-killer** — John Bain, Aurora, Ontario
- **vegecutioner** — Ian Ross, Calgary
- **veggiscarian** — Vern Yoshida, Nanaimo, British Columbia
- **vegicidal maniac** — Derek Broughton, St. Thomas, Ontario

Some listeners even confessed to being **herbicidal maniacs** themselves:

"A friend with a green thumb furnished me with a thriving spider plant. She chose the location for appropriate light, and even promised to feed it for me. All I had to do was keep the little ceramic automatic waterer topped up. I did. But soon each delicate leaf tip turned yellow . . . then brown.

The foliage dried up and shrank back. In a last desperate bid for survival, the dying plant sent out little escape pods. Miniature spiders were thrust out on long stems, far from the mother ship. They parachuted down, in the hope, I suppose, of finding a new and better world.

They looked so cheerful and optimistic, perched on the kitchen lino. Alas, they, too, learned that every scrap of decorative greenery that has the ill-fortune to enter my home is merely compost-in-training."

— *Veronica Morley Hubert*

Hosteria

Noun:

the dread of hosting a party, due to an intense
fear of social failure.

Submitted by Jeffrey Jakaitis, Oakville, Ontario

Parties may be fun to attend, but they're the source of angst and despair for most people who give them. **Hosteria** is the perfect word for this situation. What else would you call the inevitable bickering that goes on between co-hosts just before the guests arrive, or the emotional meltdown that besets those who serve the bruschetta a tad soggy? Nevertheless, parties almost always achieve lift-off. As hosts, we really should be concentrating on securing the breakables and making sure people are not taking swigs out of beer bottles that have been used for ashtrays.

Here are a few more names for those pre-party jitters:

- **enterpaining** — Cindy Ellison, Winnipeg
- **fauxpasphobic** — Louis Quigley, Riverview, New Brunswick
- **fêtetrepidation** — Steve Doran, Boise, Idaho
- **flopaphobia** — Chuck and Sue Mercer, Napanee, Ontario
- **fretiquette** — Lynn Schellenberg, Stratford, Ontario
- **friendzy** — Kevin O'Brien, Cornwall, Prince Edward Island
- **hospfatality** — Myles Ferrie, Shawnigan Lake, British Columbia
- **hosterics** — Becky Schneiderman, Halifax
- **hostress** — Alan Anderson, Paradise Hill, Saskatchewan
- **partache** — Katie Zettler, Portage la Prairie, Manitoba
- **partyac arrest** — Al Loeppky, Winkler, Alberta
- **partyduress** — Jo Anne Gerrard, Renfrew, Ontario
- **partygeist** — Jonathan Wheatcroft, Ottawa
- **partynoia** — Cathy Camp, Queen Charlotte Islands, British Columbia

- **sociojitters** — Anne Mackinnon, Keswick, Ontario
- **soirache** — Samantha Rasmussen, Neustadt, Ontario
- **sweatiquette** — Greg and Michele Landry, Sydney River, Nova Scotia

FYI

Some urban myths have extraordinary staying power, like this little recipe for **hosteria**. This imaginative tale has

evidently been circulating since the glory days of luncheon gelatin moulds, a gastronomic manoeuvre that is ill-advised in more ways than one.

A relative of (insert name of a friend of a friend here) just moved to a new town and decided to host a lunch for her new neighbours and friends. She planned the menu down to every detail and was eager to make a good impression on her guests. Just before they were due to arrive, she placed the main dish, a salmon luncheon mould, in the centre of the dining-room table. She left the room for a moment, and when she returned, her cat was eating the salmon mould. She threw the cat out and, with nothing else to serve the guests, hastily repaired the damage and rearranged the parsley.

The guests came and the party was a great success. People loved the food and the conversation was lively.

When the hostess was putting out the garbage later that afternoon, she found her cat lying in the backyard. It was dead. She phoned her doctor, who said they couldn't take any chances. It looked like food poisoning. She was instructed to call everybody from the party and tell them to get to the hospital immediately and have their stomachs pumped.

As she was returning from the hospital after her own stomach pumping, a neighbour who didn't attend the party came out to meet her. He informed her that he had accidentally run over her cat earlier that day. He had noticed that she was having a party and hadn't wanted to disturb her, or her guests, with the bad news. Instead, he had placed the cat in the backyard and decided there was no harm in telling her later.

Icekaputs

Noun:

a perilous dance performed inadvertently on ice or
hard-packed snow.

Submitted by Jamal Kazi, Knowlesville, New Brunswick

Argentina has the tango, Italy has the tarantella, and
Canada has the **icekaputs**. It's a hand-waving, leg-kicking,
anti-gravity ice dance. Frankly, we think it should be an
Olympic sport. Think about it: an **icekaput** is a demanding
athletic feat and a sight to behold. A perfect score would be
awarded only to **icekaput** sequences that include a slip, a
dance, a close-call fall, and a beautiful recovery. It can even
work as a synchronized sport. Our climate gives us a natural
edge over many countries, and it will put us back on the
Winter Olympic map. Go, team, go.

Linda Aug of Burnaby, British Columbia, asked us to
find this word. Here's the short list of other listener
suggestions:

- **asscapades** — Cristina Greco, Sudbury, Ontario
- **dance of the sore bum fairies** — Russ Hopper, Salisbury,
  New Brunswick
- **the floptrot** — Brad Perrin, Nipawin, Saskatchewan
- **frost trot** — The Matteys, Perth Road Village, Ontario
- **frostbury flop** — Dave Belovich, Nepean, Ontario
- **gyricescoping** — Len Edwards, Calgary
- **the hailmary hop** — Nick Haramis, Gloucester, Ontario
- **hopsicle** — Judie Marsden, Stittsville, Ontario
- **iceland fling** — M. J. Dickson, Peterborough, Ontario
- **icenastics** — Kevin Blanchard, Brandon, Manitoba
- **perpendiculate** — Gregory Alan Elliott, Toronto
- **skiggle** — Lionel Cook, Edmonton
- **slidewalk** — Aubrey Kissoon, Whitby, Ontario
- **slip-tease** — Phyllis Anderson, Alliston, Ontario

- **squirmafrost** — Vern Yoshida, Nanaimo, British Columbia
- **triple klutz** — John Corbett, Toronto
- **weebling** — D. M. Drew

FYI

A note about slipjigs: This was the most common suggestion for this Wanted Word. It's a word for a fast Irish jig where the dancer sticks his legs out at odd angles and dances furiously in front of the beat. It's hard enough to do on dry land, let alone frozen ground. Maybe the cast members of *Riverdance* will consider staging a command performance of the **icekaputs** on the Rideau Canal in January.

Immaculate Correction

Noun:

the spontaneous act of a computer or other
machine fixing itself as soon as a repair person arrives.
Submitted by John Jorgenson, Huntsville, Ontario

Now here's a word that had people nodding with recognition. Everyone seemed to have a hairy little tale about a machine or a computer that likes to pretend it's broken. Of course, **immaculate corrections** are not limited to inanimate objects — our bodies routinely fix themselves while seated in doctor's offices. But while every help-desk expert claims that human errors are at the root of all malfunctions, every human we heard from agrees that more mysterious forces are at play.

Here's the short list of other brilliant suggestions:

- **autofixation** — Carl Hird-Rutter, Chilliwack, British Columbia
- **cofixidence** — Kevin Shipley, Kingston, Ontario
- **devil ex machina** — Shelley Mahoney
- **expertease** — Ellen Watt, Edmonton
- **farcefield** — Cindy and Rob Brownlee, North Bay, Ontario
- **metafixical** — David L. Henteleff, Winnipeg
- **nostradammit** — Guy Wilton, Ladner, British Columbia
- **phantasmaglitch** — Mary Anderson, St. Louis Park, Minnesota
- **polterglitch** — Simon Wood, Hamilton, Ontario
- **precognitronics** — John Spence, Toronto
- **precovery** — Averell Sherker, Montreal
- **premature capitulation** — Chris Corrigan, Vancouver
- **problemnotic** — Sherry Wykes, Brandon, Manitoba
- **proxifix** — Heather Kobayakawa, Markham, Ontario
- **repairadox** — Paul Reilly
- **repairanoia** — Maurice Hogue, Winnipeg

- **repairanormal** — Sandra Waines, Huntsville, Ontario
- **serenfixity** — Alan Crarer, Vancouver
- **technochondria** — Karl Tribe, Apohaqui, New Brunswick

FYI

Quantum bogodynamics is a theory that alpha-geeks have come up with to explain why **immaculate corrections** occur. It's a little hard to follow (not unlike the instruction manual for a VCR), but the notion that "suits" are the source of negative "bogon" vibrations is oddly compelling.

quantum bogodynamics / kwon'tm boh`goh-di:-nam'iks / n. A theory that characterizes the universe in terms of bogon sources (such as politicians, used-car salesmen, TV evangelists, and suits in general), bogon sinks (such as taxpayers and computers), and potential bogosity fields. Bogon absorption, of course, causes human beings to behave mindlessly and machines to fail (and may also cause both to emit secondary bogons); however, the precise mechanics of the bogon-computron interaction are not yet understood and remain to be elucidated. Quantum bogodynamics is most often invoked to explain the sharp increase in hardware and software failures in the presence of suits; the latter emit bogons, which the former absorb.

Source: *The Jargon Dictionary*

Indian Bummer

Noun:

the blast of winter that comes after the first few days
of spring warmth; the opposite of an Indian summer.
Submitted by Jeff Osweiler, Montreal

Here's the situation: There's been a full week of warm weather; the grass is green, leaves are popping out of their buds, and the squirrels have shed their mangy winter coats. By all estimates, spring has sprung. So you throw on a pair of shorts, clean up the barbecue, put out the lawn furniture, and, best of all, put away the snow shovels and road salt. You go to sleep that night happy and just a little bit sunburned. But you wake up to the nightmare that is **Indian bummer**. Thirty centimetres of snow have fallen, roads are closed, and the power is out. Whether you're roughing it in the bush or taking the subway downtown, this inclement time warp is enough to make you pray for global warming.

According to several listeners who wrote in, **Indian bummer** is known in Newfoundland as Sheila's Brush. It is a sudden reversion to severe winter weather around St. Paddy's Day, and it's named after St. Patrick's sister or mother or aunt. Heck, maybe it was his cleaning lady. Anyway, as the story goes, fishermen used to wait out Sheila's Brush before venturing out to the spring ice floes. That didn't stop lots of listeners west of Newfoundland from coming up with a wonderful array of new words, including:

- **coldslap** — Gwen Casey, Mt. Albert, Ontario
- **crocuspocus** — Marilyn Stratton, Calgary
- **equinox pox** — Robert O'Donnell, New Glasgow, Nova Scotia
- **equinoxious** — Doug McLaughlin, Calgary
- **fool's cold** — Katherine Aldred, Ottawa
- **frostspite** — Isabelle Eaton, Vernon, British Columbia
- **snowscorn** — Ken Ernhofer

- **snowvertime**
  — Karl Christian, Tilden Lake, Ontario
- **spring claw**
  — Nancy Van Patten, Saltspring Island, British Columbia
- **spring flaw**
  — Konrad Ejbich, Toronto
- **spring fraud**
  — Ric Dolphin, Edmonton

- **spring-pong**
  — Rick Harby, Winnipeg
- **warmageddon** — Robert Tetu, Seaforth, Ontario
- **white blight** — Michael Nesbitt, Prince Edward Island

Interangst

Noun:

the waiting period between swiping your credit or debit card and getting approved or denied by the bank.

Submitted by Joanna McGarvie, Ucluelet, British Columbia

Interac and debit cards have brought a lot of changes to the simple act of buying things — most notably, the agony and the ecstasy of swipestakes. This is the spine-tingling game of chance you play when you don't know how much money you have in your bank account, but you load up on groceries anyway.

In the days when cash prevailed, you could always put being "a bit short" down to bad math skills or forgetfulness (i.e., "I forgot my wallet"). But electronic debit cards hack right into your bank balance and pull up the hard facts of your financial status — or lack thereof. Refusal means double humiliation — once in front of the sales clerk, and then again in front of the whole lineup. Despite these perils, which have us swiperventilating, Canadians are smitten with swiping. Between 1994 and 1998, debit card use exploded by 630 percent, according to Interac, Canada's electronic funds-transfer network. Our purchases added up to a total of $58.5 billion in 1998 alone. That's a lot of **interangst**.

Here's the short list of other suggestions:

- **apoplastic** — David Sweetnam
- **bangst** — Jack Stewart, Sackville, New Brunswick
- **bankxiety** — Sylvia Legris, Saskatchewan
- **buyatus** — David Walker, Grimsby, Ontario
- **credilude** — Ken Snider, Dawson City, Yukon
- **debiternity** — Bob Felker, Ayr, Ontario
- **fundticipation** — Lucille Carter, Alexandra, Prince Edward Island
- **interache** — Ian Brookes, Toronto
- **moneypause** — Silas Barss Donham, Whycocomagh, Nova Scotia
- **pay-delay** — Barbara Linklater, Winnipeg
- **paygatory** — Vince Panzica, Bolton, Ontario
- **pinterlude** — Jack Orchard
- **pintermission** — Scott Turner, Vancouver
- **purcardtory** — Vic Hamilton, Salmon Arm, British Columbia
- **purchasetory** — Andrew Fitzpatrick, St. John's
- **sangfroid-plastique** — C. J. Orole, Gravenhurst, Ontario
- **splurgeatory** — Pat Weiss, Winnipeg
- **swangst** — Kahente Horn-Miller, Kahnawake, Quebec
- **swipeout** — David Kidd, Dawson Creek, British Columbia
- **swipertension** — Cathie Henderson, Toronto
- **swiperventilate** — Debbie Sayers, Tuktoyaktuk, Northwest Territories
- **swipestakes** — Leslie Johnson, Callander, Ontario

Line-Whine

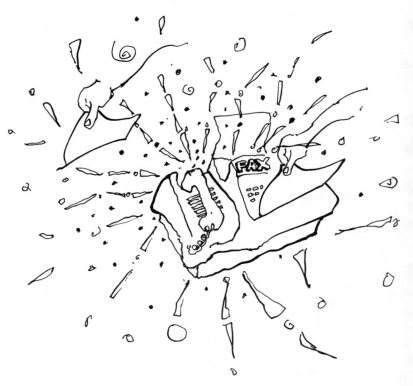

Noun:

the noise made by two modems when they are negotiating
what speed and form their digital conversation will take.

Submitted by Nancy Houghton-Larue, Sainte-Foy, Quebec

Line-whine is the painful soundtrack you're subjected to whenever you send e-mails or faxes. Computer technicians in the know inform us that the piercing screech and squawk of a modem already has a name — it's an electronic handshake, a digital negotiation.

We wondered what it would look like if we sent two fax/modems on a hot digital date:

"Hello. I'd like to communicate with you at 56K baud."

"But, honey, I can handle only 28K tonight."

"Why don't you come on over and get a little upgrade?"

So we have only one question, Mr. Alpha-geek: If cellphones can play Beethoven, why can't modems play anything a little less grating than **line-whine**?

Here's what some other listeners called it:

- **chip chirp** — Bob Mortimer, Renfrew, Ontario
- **faxerwauling** — Doug Hill, Cornwall, Ontario
- **faxetto** — Sylvia Legris, Saskatchewan
- **faxophony** — Karen Herzberger, Don Mills, Ontario
- **faxsquawk** — Joanne Jackson Johnson, Whitehorse, Yukon
- **greech** — Alex Lopez-Ortiz, Fredericton
- **hyper-dingle** — Hugh Rogerson, Harley, Ontario
- **infoscreech** — Kate Hahnen, Montreal
- **modem yodel** — Doc G., Windsor, Ontario
- **netscrape** — Darren Heroux, Montreal
- **screaming faxshee** — Lysa Bertoli, Toronto
- **screeching out** — Gord Lindsay, Toronto
- **song of the modem bird** — Bennett McCardle, Toronto

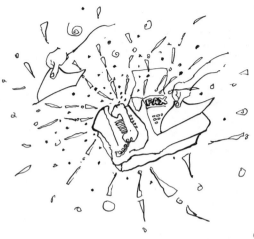

- **squall forwarding** — Brian McHugh, Corner Brook, Newfoundland
  - **squeep** — Matthew Gariss, Quebec
  - **squeerch** B. J. Milner
- **tron song** Hugh Matheson, Gaspé, Quebec
- **turkeygobble** — Andrew Tremayne
- **viletone** — Tom Hutchinson, McBride, British Columbia

Motorolamouth

Noun:

someone who engages in the loud and obnoxious
use of cellphones in public places.

Submitted by Aleck Skeie and Barry Smith

Glen Dias of Stratford, Ontario, got us started on this word search, which clearly tapped into some intense feelings of frustration on the part of listeners. Cellphones are a wonderful invention, but why do the people who own them come down with an instant case of **motorolamouth** when they use them in public? Is there some reason why a normal human being would pick up a phone and call a friend to say, "I'm in 7-Eleven right now. What flavour of breath mints should I buy?" And is there any way we can escape all this mind-numbing blather?

Well, in fact, relief is on the way, in the form of an anti-cellphone movement. Inspired by the belligerence of cellevangelists and imbecells, a growing number of restaurants, theatres, churches, funeral homes, workplaces, buses, trains, parks, and schools have banned cellphones. Nine countries — Japan, England, Sweden, Switzerland, Spain, Australia, Israel, Italy, and Singapore — have banned or limited the use of cellphones while driving, reflecting concern that cellphone use in cars increases the likelihood of collisions. Despite this, high-tech firms have plans to manufacture other attention-getting dashboard gadgets such as fax machines, televisions, and computers.

It all has some people madder than a grid-locked cabbie. Americans Tom and Ray Magliozzi are the poster boys for the campaign to rid highways of cellphone-using drivers. As hosts of the popular National Public Radio show "Car Talk," they have hit a nerve with their Drive Now, Talk Later campaign and bumper stickers (more than sixty thousand have been distributed). They say that drivers face too many distractions as it is, and that having cellphones in cars is "stupid and crazy."

Our listeners appear to agree, as this inventive short list of suggestions attests:

- **bellbarians** — Rene Jamieson, Winnipeg
- **call-watch-me** — Vern Yoshida, Nanaimo, British Columbia
- **cell-centred** — Laurel Kreuger, Baker Lake, Nunavut
- **cell-droids** — Ron Henschel, Greenwood, British Columbia
- **cellevangelist** — A. J. McKechnie, Toronto
- **celliloquy** — Robert Burnell, Sainte-Foy, Quebec
- **cellots** — Rick Callahan, St. John's
- **cellphonedulgent** — Robert and Rebekah Garfat, Cobble Hill, British Columbia
- **imbecell** — Randal Corran, Vancouver
- **jabberwalking** — Donna McLaughlin, Sparwood, British Columbia
- **phonetificating** — Bob Ellison, Yellowknife, Northwest Territories
- **roamin' warriors** — Owen and Cass Torode, Vancouver
- **show-and-cell** — Don MacDonald, Brantford, Ontario
- **talkie-jockey** — David Carroll, Richmond Hill, Ontario
- **telebarketer** — Brian Gaudet, Halifax
- **telefoons** — Dan Dingee, Trenton, Ontario
- **walkingspiel** — Russ Collins, Escuminac, Quebec
- **yell-phone** — Melissa and Andrew Chapman

Here's an anti-motorolamouth poem that was sent in by Linda Smith and her daughter, Octavia Bermbach, from Summerland, British Columbia:

On a city street, in an airport lounge,
It's for this word we listeners scrounge.
What to call that guy who's prone
To barking shrilly at his phone?
Such blatant lack of cell-oquence
Grates on our ears and makes us tense.

"I'm in Starbucks now," he yells,
Amplifying all he tells.
His waving arms, his promenading,
Make you think he must be trading
With his broker, client or other,
When he's really talking to his mother.

Who is this man who loves to rant?
Some would say a cello-phant.
Who tells the whole word where he's at?
I'd say he's called a cell-abrat.
But underneath all that baloney,
This guy is just a cello-phoney.

Mudlash

Noun:

the streak of water and mud that
identifies a cyclist who rides in the rain
without a fender.

Submitted by Kim McLean-Fiander, Lethbridge, Alberta

Mudlash

We were tipped off to this Wanted Word by Krystal Mack-Kiley of Kingston, Ontario. People unfamiliar with the perils of riding modern bicycles struggle to understand what this word means. They probably lived in a bygone era when mud flaps and fenders were standard equipment on bicycles. Poor things — how they must envy the spinstripe suits of commuting cyclists. These proud bearers of road-skunk know that a soggy backside and a thick stripe of greasy road gack on their business attire are a small price to pay to avoid the humiliation of spending ten dollars on wheel fenders.

Here's the short list of other listener suggestions:

- **back splash** — Chris Molloy, Lumby, British Columbia
- **back splat** — Sandra Blaxland, LaHave, Nova Scotia
- **backtrack** — Wendy Stewart, Calgary
- **bicycle-butt** — Corina Brdar, Edmonton
- **biker-butt** — Cynthia Graham, Calgary
- **cycline** — Linda Langman, Oro Station, Ontario
- **dorsal gripe** — Debbie Hazlewood, Hamilton, Ontario

- **fendirt** — Jane Jacques, Fort McMurray, Alberta
- **gritspine** — Lulu Mannseichner, Oxford Mills, Ontario
- **hindstripe** — Eric Coates, Stratford, Ontario
- **Pepe Le Spew** — Roger Dunkley, Calgary
- **road-skunked** — Michael Armstrong, Prince George, British Columbia
- **roostertail** — Monica Webster, Calgary
- **skidder** — Mac Fenwick, Peterborough, Ontario
- **skunckle** — Marianne Moershel, Madoc, Ontario
- **spinfin** — Michael Keohan
- **spinstripe suit** — Carl Jorgenson, Sudbury, Ontario
- **splack** — Jim Plaxton, Toronto
- **street-streak** — Kathy Kerr, Meaford, Ontario
- **trek-drek** — Fall River Village People, Windsor Junction, Nova Scotia
- **vertespray** — Jack Stewart, Sackville, New Brunswick

N

Namenesia

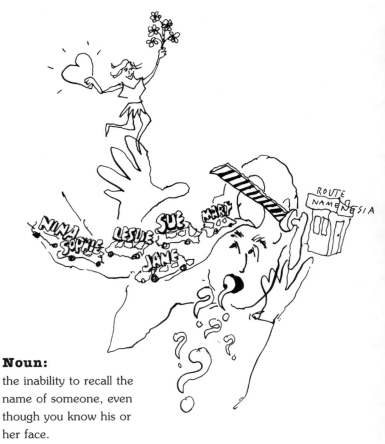

Noun:

the inability to recall the name of someone, even though you know his or her face.

Submitted by Pat Brown, Sidney, British Columbia

Scientists call this syndrome "prosopanomia" — a word that won't come to mind easily when you're struggling with a bout of **Namenesia**. This is a common phenomenon to say the least, and it's particularly embarrassing when it happens with people you know quite well, such as co-workers and close friends. Here's the short list of listener suggestions:

- **déjà su** — Gilles Gautreau, Rothesay, New Brunswick
- **déjà who** — Melodie Cook, Ottawa
- **fuginym** — Nancy Van Patten, Saltspring Island, British Columbia
- **memory gasp** — Jamal Kazi, Knowlesville, New Brunswick
- **mug bug** — Rafe McNabb, Chemainus, British Columbia
- **name-drain** — Lalage Morka, Chezzetcook, Nova Scotia
- **nom du blank** — Wendy Bateman, Bluehawk Lake, Ontario
- **nomblivion** — Jennifer O'Rourke, Gabriola Island, British Columbia
- **nomenblankture** — Phyllis Jacklin, Toronto
- **nomeseizure** — Elizabeth Becker, King City, Ontario

FYI

According to Jean Saint-Cyr, an associate professor in surgery and psychology at the University of Toronto, names are hard to remember partly because they are unique information items. There are multiple routes and links to general information items, but the path in the brain used to retrieve an item as specific as somebody's name is extremely narrow or limited. If anything disturbs your attempt to tag a face with a name, that processing path will be vulnerable and hard to retrace. Despite this, people are very good at putting a name to a face, even if they've only been exposed to it briefly.

Napsnap

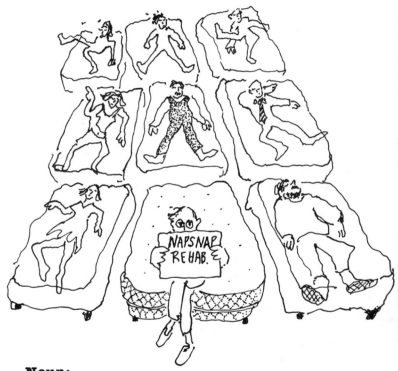

Noun:

the full body twitch and jerk that often snaps a person out of sleep just as he or she is drifting off. Sometimes accompanied by a dream of falling or colliding with something.

Submitted by Ludvick Prevec, Burlington, Ontario

Napsnap is a massive body twitch that often doesn't
wake the sleeper, but almost certainly rouses (or maims) the
person he or she is sleeping with. Pity the poor spouses of
NHL goalies who get to nuzzle up to snookums while he's
dreaming of making a split save in seventh game of the
Stanley Cup finals. **Napsnap** occurs early on in a night's
sleep, but it is not to be confused with the drowsy head-
bobbing that usually accompanies late-night TV watching or
university lectures. Roger Dunkley of Calgary put us onto this
search, and here's the short list:

- **naplash** — Doug Bowes, Victoria
- **narcospasm** — Andrew MacGregor, Boulder, Colorado
- **pajamawhamma** — Rick Callahan, St. John's
- **sack-whack** — Brent Kolbeck, Emerald Park,
  Saskatchewan
- **shake 'n' wake** — Shelley and Ron Kary, Wetaskiwin,
  Alberta
- **slapnea** — Bernadette Arsenault, New Brunswick
- **sleep spasnia** — Catherine Cole, Huntsville, Ontario
- **sleepjerky** — Lisa Hann, New Brunswick
- **sleeplash** — Greta Descantes, Halifax
- **sleepleap** — Nancy Love, Toronto
- **slerk** — Randy Mugford, Halifax
- **slumberbomb** — Mark Mazerolle, Winnipeg
- **slumberjerk** — Heather Boyle, Tsawwassen,
  British Columbia
- **slumberjolt** — Roy MacLachlan, Fawcett, Alberta
- **snapnea** — Rick Barker, Vancouver

- **snooze-goose** — Joy Strickland, Victoria
- **snoozure** — John David Gravenor, Montreal
- **snoregasm** — David Wagener, Caledonia, Nova Scotia
- **sonambunudge** — Sarah Mainguy, Aberfoyle, Ontario
- **spousespaz** — Vern Yoshida, Nanaimo, British Columbia

Napsnap was a familiar phenomenon to listeners, many of whom wrote to tell us more about their experiences:

"I was quite surprised to find out that my husband did this incredible body twitch when falling asleep. I married him in 1977, the same year *Star Wars* came out. In it, there was a scene about making the leap into hyperspace, and somehow the two ideas connected. Ever since then, we've been calling this jerking thing the 'sleepleap.' My husband's sleepleap is so violent I had to develop my own strategy for falling asleep. I wait until he has sleptleapt before I drift off."

— *Nancy Love, Toronto*

FYI

Scientists have a few choice words for **napsnap** — the myoclonic jerk and the hypnic jerk. The tweedle-dee and tweedle-dum of sleep twitches are a natural part of the body's metamorphosis from alertness to a restorative sleep state. Breathing slows, body temperature drops, and muscles relax. Some scientists believe the hypnic/myoclonic jerks are merely a by-product of the body's relaxing in this manner — leftover lactic acids act like carbon build-up on your car's engine cylinders and cause run-on.

But there's a much more exotic theory in circulation that has to do with genetic memory and our swingin' genetic forebears. Basically, we draw a lot of our genetic code from tree-dwelling animals, and these cousins of ours don't fare too well if they fall out of their beds a couple of hundred feet up in the forest canopy. Some scientists conclude that the hypnic/myoclonic jerk is an ancient instinctual warning system embedded in our DNA that alerts us to the hazard of allowing our muscles to relax a little too much. "Wake up, you're losing your grip," the brain screams to the body. This also explains why these jerks are often accompanied by dreams of falling.

P

Le Peur Noel

Noun: the dread and anxiety you feel the first time you hear Christmas music in a mall or on a TV commercial.

Submitted by Genevieve Willis, Ottawa

88

Now let's make one thing clear: you don't have to be a Grinch to suffer from **Le Peur Noel**. It can happen to even the most fervent fans of all things Christmas. But even the Bible says that "to all things there is a season," and let's face it, late October is not the season to be hearing "The Little Drummer Boy." Can we please get through Halloween at least? Yes, the Christmas season is important to retailers, and yes, Christmas music seems to put us in a buying mood, but we always get around to buying those presents eventually, so let's just relax and not send us into fits of anxiety before it's absolutely necessary.

Here are some of the other great words suggested by our listeners:

- **chrispepsia** — Karen Herzberger, Don Mills, Ontario
- **Do You Fear What I Fear?** — George Duquette, North Bay, Ontario
- **the drelves** — Kara Massie, Galiano Island, British Columbia
- **festiphobia** — Lorna Lynch, Kaslo, British Columbia
- **The First Oh-Hell** — Robert Hepple, Winnipeg
- **Grinch glinch** — John Nursall, Calgary
- **Handel's Nausiah** — Rick Williams, Halifax
- **hohophobia** — Lorna Rowsell, Calgary
- **Jingle Blahs** — Maurice Hogue, Winnipeg
- **jingle jangles** — Sandy Ebbs, Black Sturgeon Lake, Ontario
- **Nutcracker Sweat** — Marcy Slapcoff, Montreal
- **paniclaus** — Jamal Kazi, Knolesville, New Brunswick

- **panicsmas**
  — Vickie Kayuk,
    Dunrobin, Ontario
- **Rudolph's revenge**
  — Peter Faris, Calgary
- **Santa Affective Disorder (SAD)**
  — Peter de Kadelbach and
    Paula Ferreira, Montreal
- **Santaclobbered**
  — Glen Bragg, Calgary

Playdirt

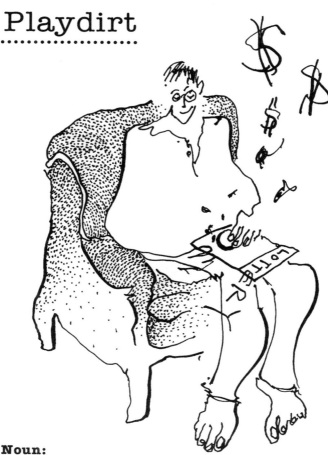

Noun:

the waxy rubbings that come off
lottery tickets when they're scratched.

Submitted by Paul Kearley, Sussex, New Brunswick

Gary Ockenden of Nelson, British Columbia, and Gary Langille of Halifax asked us to come up with a word for those rubbery shavings that remain after you've played a scratch-and-lose lottery game. Lotteries have been called a tax on the stupid. The purpose behind this particular type of game appears to be that it allows you to postpone the inevitable. Instead of becoming just another "instant loser," you get to spend an extra 3.5 seconds (slightly longer if you use your fingernail) fantasizing about what may lie underneath that thin layer of **playdirt**. Stupid? What do you think? Just remember to clean up your mess.

Here are some of the other words suggested by our listeners:

- **dimegrime** — Jason Murdoch, Hamilton, Ontario
- **exfooliation** — Stephanie Chambers, Toronto
- **gambules** — Ken Turner, Rossland, British Columbia
- **gratch** — Tony Chander, Sidney, British Columbia
- **loser lint** — Gary Ockenden, Nelson, British Columbia
- **lotto-boogers** — Gen Keen, Sudbury, Ontario
- **lotto-lint** — Melissa Tichborne, West St. Paul, Manitoba
- **lust bunnies** — Suzanne Thorson, Kingston, Ontario
- **rubbishes** — Jill Laudin, Brunkild, Manitoba
- **scratchanscree** — J. Gerry Mugford, St. John's
- **scratchels** — Fred Schaub, Sorrento, British Columbia
- **scratchins** — Katya Androsoff, Calgary
- **scritchins** — Margaret Longthorp, Saint John, New Brunswick
- **scrud** — Gini Walsh, Victoria

- **suckerdust** — Leo Sampson, Dartmouth, Nova Scotia
- **sweep scrapes** — Michael Evans, Regina
- **tryagrains** — Greg Landry, Sydney River, Nova Scotia

"My older brother Monty buys a scratch-and-win ticket pretty well every day," writes Sandy Ockenden of Victoria. "He takes it home, sits in his favourite chair, and savours the moment, scratch by scratch. The particular place where he sits is getting rather dusty. When asked about it, my brother always replies, with a knowing tone, 'That's not any dust — that's dream-dust. And when there's enough of it, my dreams will come true.' Monty's expression has always stuck with me."

FYI

What is **playdirt** anyway? The play area of these lottery tickets is painted over with a latex coating. Though many people have tried, the coating cannot be X-rayed or deciphered to determine which tickets are winners. Bingo and Crossword are the most popular scratch games, and they are slightly more popular with women than with men.

Pokemound

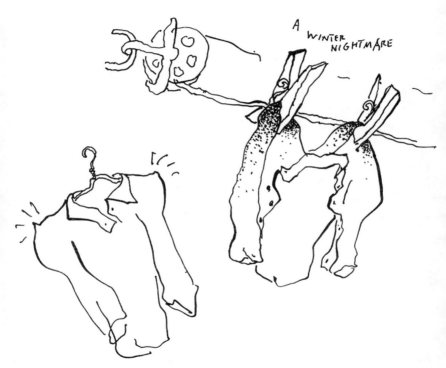

A WINTER NIGHTMARE

Noun:

the indentation a hanger, hook, or clothespin
makes in the shoulders of shirts and jackets.

Submitted by William Fraser, Vancouver

Like the word "bagmata" before it, **pokemound** closes a very small but important gap in the English language. Zelda Norman kicked off this Wanted Word search with this letter: "I was at a party where one of the guests was wearing a turtleneck shirt with the hanger bumps showing. He was unaware of these bumps sitting on top of each shoulder. We'd love to have a name for them."

And here's the short list:

- **bink** — Dave White, Falconbridge, Ontario
- **closet camel** — Krystal Mack-Kiley, Kingston, Ontario
- **gnurble** — Rob Janzen, St. Catharines, Ontario
- **hanger horn** — Lassi Tuomialho, Thunder Bay, Ontario
- **hangerfang** — Toon Pronk, Fredericton
- **hangerhump** — T. Kelly, Burlington, Ontario
- **himple** — James Brown, Victoria
- **humptybump** — Phil Salem, Sioux Lookout, Ontario
- **layaway lump** — A gaggle of seven- to ten-year-olds from the Junior Writer's Club in Cambridge, Ontario
- **lumple** — Jill Hefley
- **napex** — Yanik Richards, Charlottetown
- **pook** — Jeanette and Gary O'Reilly, Charlottetown
- **Quasimoda** — Colin MacDonald, Barrie, Ontario
- **shoulder pod** — Anonymous
- **suspendent** — Deepika Grover, Toronto
- **tweedbump** — Barry Mulvaney, Vernon, British Columbia

"When our children were young, we used to live in Smithers, in the central interior of British Columbia," write Miriam and

Doug Faris of Hornby Island, British Columbia. "They were frequently piqued by our practice of putting the laundry out on the line to dry in the dead of winter. Their clothing froze solid, but did in fact dry — wonder of wonders. However, when these 'board shirts' were brought in and thawed out, they ended up with little horns on each shoulder from the clothespins. They coined the term 'soldier shoulders' to describe the phenomenon."

FYI

The word search for **pokemound** brought us face to face with a crucial social dilemma: What is the etiquette surrounding the stigma of **pokemounds**? Do you sidle up to the person and tweak the bumps surreptitiously, or just pretend they're not there? Kids are much clearer on **pokemound** social behaviour — point, stare, and ridicule peers in the schoolyard. Maybe we can take a page from their etiquette book when dealing with those little bits of food that get stuck in people's teeth or beards.

Polkadodge

Noun:

the subtle dance two strangers engage in when trying to move
past each other on a sidewalk or in a hallway.

Submitted by Katie Wood, Lively, Ontario

Several prominent lexicographers have taken a stab at this phenomenon. The Canadian wordmeister Bill Casselman calls it an "indecisijig." Douglas Adams, author of *The Meaning of Liff*, calls it a "droitwich." And the American comic Rich Hall, of Sniglets fame (words that don't appear in the dictionary but should), has coined the word "youfirstics." All of these are worthwhile contributions to the English language, but nothing has stuck with those who reach for this word on an almost daily basis. Ultimately, we're looking to the United Nations for help on this one. Until there is an international agreement governing the direction two people should take as they head towards each other on a sidewalk, the **polkadodge** will continue to be the world's most popular dance. And if you happen to duck into a doorway to avoid a collision, you could say you've encountered a **polkadodge** door. You could say that . . . but we advise against it.

Here are some other possibilities:

- **avoidance** — Murray Hagen, Prince Albert, Saskatchewan
- **bossa no va** — Adam Levin, Toronto
- **dorky-dancing** — Doug Speers, Summerland, British Columbia
- **faux trot** — Catherine Elstone, Elmira, Ontario
- **hesidance** — Mike Nagy, Rockwood, Ontario
- **hobble-wobble** — Karen Harding, Richmond Hill, Ontario
- **polka-duck** — Nancy McLennan, Wellman Lake, Manitoba
- **sidewaltz** — Cindy Nicholls, Paris, Ontario
- **sidewinder waltz** — The Allen family
- **sidewuffle** — Alison Thorne, St. John's
- **steptease** — Neil Schroeter, Pemberton, British Columbia
- **stop 'n' hop** — David Breckenridge, Sault Ste. Marie, Ontario
- **stopscotch** — Isabel Blackledge, Whitefish Falls, Ontario
- **struffle** — Heidi den Haan, Portage la Prairie, Manitoba
- **walkstrot** — Barbara Michaelsen, Newmarket, Ontario

P

Ponis

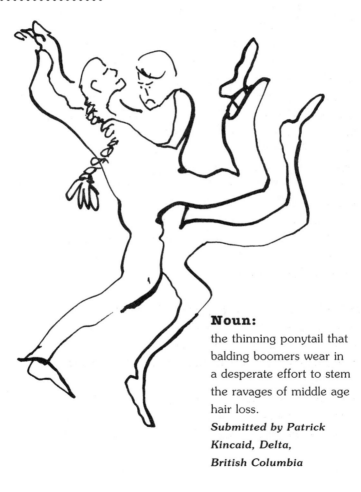

Noun:

the thinning ponytail that balding boomers wear in a desperate effort to stem the ravages of middle age hair loss.

Submitted by Patrick Kincaid, Delta, British Columbia

Think of Jack Nicholson in *The Witches of Eastwick*.
Think of George Carlin or any member of Crosby, Stills, Nash
& Young. Think of the fake ponytail that Steve Martin would
strap on when he wanted to impress Hollywood moguls in
Bowfinger. Think of the aging boomers you find in health-
food shops or second-hand bookstores, fingering their
scraggly little phonytails just to make sure there is still
something there. Not a pretty picture, is it?

The **ponis** is similar in some ways to the mullet or the
ape drape — the "short on the top, long on the back" hairdo
favoured by hockey players and bad country singers. Some
call this phoney-tail a "skullet," like Daniel Grisdale of Alberta,
who says that "whereas the mullet is 'business in the front,
party in the back,' the skullet is through with business, and it's
just party, party, party."

But we decided to call it a **ponis**. You either get it or
you don't. You either love it or you don't. We love it.

Here are some of the more than one thousand suggestions
submitted by our listeners:

- **baldielocks** — Gerri Brightwell, Winnipeg
- **baldman's bluff** — Judie Marsden, Stittsville, Ontario
- **boomer-bang** — Ellen Gonza, Fredericton
- **desperadoo** — Lu Bob Mannseichner, Oxford Mills,
  Ontario
- **dome-mane** — Gino Palumbo
- **Don Juan-a-bee** — Mark Loeppky, Winkler, Manitoba
- **Don Juan-a-do** — Adrian DiGiuseppe, Thunder Bay,
  Ontario

- **dork-handle** — Geoff Wilkinson, Tsawwassen,
  British Columbia
- **dork-knob** — Maggi Williams, Chelsea, Quebec
- **folic symbol** — Brenda Daoust, Coquitlam,
  British Columbia
- **hippy-gripper** — Vern Yoshida, Nanaimo, British Columbia
- **hoperope** — Anita Dougherty, Prince George,
  British Columbia
- **manhandle** — Gordon Quesnelle, Port McNicoll, Ontario
- **nape-drape** — Bruce Hawn, Orillia, Ontario
- **oldielocks** — Paul Kearley, Sussex, New Brunswick
- **phonytail** — Ed Turpin, St. John's, and Patrick Couperus,
  Ottawa
- **pity tale** — Ronald MacFarlane, Fernwood,
  Prince Edward Island
- **pony excess** — Gary Miller, Fort Lauderdale, Florida
- **pullet** — Ken Tough, Monserrat
- **punytail** — Justin Baird, Vancouver
- **ratlet** — Sarah Korba, Ottawa
- **skullet** — Scott McCraw, Toronto

A remarkably good sense of humour was displayed by several listeners who admitted to having a **ponis**. This is just a small sample:

"I call it my permanent bad hair day. For the purpose of this contest, I'm going to suggest 'a bareback pony,' though it hurts me to say it."

— *Maurice Verkaar, Vancouver*

"I am fifty years old and part of the Boomer generation. I also possess one of those ponytails. In my case, my tail and beard have been a part of me since 1972, although I am a bit thinner on top than I was at twenty-two. I haven't been able to part with either. For those with nouveau ponytails to go along with their nouveau baldness, I would like to propose that they call their new appendage a vanitail."

— Hal Mitchell, Nelson, British Columbia

"I too retain a scrawny bit of fluff that is carefully and proudly tied back. There was a time when my flowing, golden locks cascaded around my youthful head, but after years of abuse, my pride and joy gradually thinned out and 'disaphaired.' This little thing that hangs down the back of my neck is all I have left. It grows about an inch a year, so I figure in about five years I will again feel it tickle me between the shoulder blades. I realize of course that I must look like an anemic pony, but it feels good to have something growing up there. How about this word — the lastclasp?"

— Jed Hiltz, Port Sydney, Ontario

Powernoia

Noun:

an irrational fear of authority, of "getting caught,"
when you have done absolutely nothing wrong.
Submitted by Noel Griffin, Vancouver

Here's the scene. You're driving back from a week's visit to the United States. You've bought about a hundred bucks worth of stuff, well within the allowable limit. Everything you bought is perfectly legal. You're inching your way up to the customs window. You're rehearsing your answers — "Canadian citizen . . . pleasure . . . one week . . . a hundred dollars" — but you can feel the sweat starting to form on your forehead. Your mouth is getting dry, and you're tightening your grip on the steering wheel. By the time you reach the window, you're a quivering, sweaty mess. When the customs officer says, "Would you mind pulling your car over there so we can have a look inside?" you feel almost relieved. At last, you can confess to your crimes — if only you could remember what they were. Sound familiar? You're experiencing a textbook case of **powernoia**.

And just so you don't think we are making this up, here's the letter from Karen Halloran-Bidlake of Penobsquis, New Brunswick, that started us on our search:

"This past Saturday evening, my husband looked up from his hockey game to comment on the fact that someone had just driven into our yard. So . . . flanked and protected by our 'vicious' German shepherds, which to this point hadn't made a sound, I went to investigate. There, in front of our garage, was a large four-wheel-drive vehicle full of RCMP officers. Even though I knew no one in the house was involved in any criminal activities, my first thought was 'My God, I'm going to be arrested.' I need a word to describe the feeling of fear and guilt that washes over an innocent person when he or she is approached by authority figures like police officers."

Here are some of the other words suggested by our listeners:

- **appretension** — Steve Taylor, Musquodoboit Harbour, Nova Scotia
- **authoriphobia** — Caleb Wong, Prince George, British Columbia
- **authoritention** — Judy Parsons Budgell, Prospect Bay, Nova Scotia
- **badgery** — Lynn Senecal, St-Lambert, Quebec
- **badgitation** — Liam Keliher, Kingston, Ontario
- **border-disorder** — The Gaunces, Saint John, New Brunswick
- **copitulation** — Sylvia Harron, Ucluelet, British Columbia
- **dreadocence** — Cornelia Howell, Lachine, Quebec
- **fuzzstration** — David Cook, Vancouver
- **guilterplexy** — Brian Smith
- **gulpable** — Jane Miller, Toronto
- **kopkaesque experience** — Hiroshi Koshiyama, Winnipeg
- **me-ah-gulpa** — Della Stoosbosscher, Waterloo, Ontario
- **pullover-sweater** — Audrey Ivimey, Kingston, Ontario
- **scrutinoia** — Nancy Van Patten, Saltspring Island, British Columbia
- **sinnocence** — Gary Disch, Aylmer, Quebec
- **sirrealism** — Joanne Dionne, Englehart, Ontario
- **trapidation** — Tina Gilbertson, New York
- **unifobia** — Paddy Fuller, Ottawa

Presqu'achoo

Noun:

a sneeze that fizzles out; an aborted sneeze (proto-sneeze?).
Submitted by Janet Bryon, Vancouver

Few bodily functions are as frustrating as the
presqu'achoo. It has all the wind-up of a regular sneeze
— the gaping mouth, the heavy breathing — but it disappears
into thin air when it's time for lift-off. It leaves you feeling
kind of ripped off, on top of congested. **Presqu'achoo**
is a perfect word for the sneeze that fizzles — and what's
more, it's bilingual. Here's the short list of other listener
suggestions:

- **adenoidance** — Don Metcalf, Waterloo, Ontario
- **eruptus interruptus** — Bob Dewar, Sudbury, Ontario
- **gesundheist** — Sheila Conlin, Toronto
- **gesundnotquite** — Anita Block, Toronto
- **noblow** — Hopewell Avenue Grade 7/8 class, Ottawa
- **nosedud** — Kate Barris
- **nostrildamus** — John Moyes, Niagara-on-the-Lake, Ontario
- **nunachu** — Roger Ross, Winnipeg
- **pas d'achoo** — Michele Sova, Kingston, Ontario
- **sneezel** — Chris Morrison, Halifax
- **sneezure** — Douglas Wilson, Victoria
- **sneezus interruptus** — Carol McKee, Dartmouth, Nova Scotia
- **snifle** — Ken Labout, Fort Resolution, Northwest Territories
- **snimplosion** — Jean Lewis, Ottawa
- **snizzle** — The Bowman family, Fredericton
- **un-choo** — Judy Wood, Saskatoon

FYI

Getting back to the science of sneezing . . . Why does our nasal-control centre abandon a perfectly good sneeze when all systems are go everywhere else? Well, sneezes are aborted because there's not enough powder to ignite the explosion. Barney Gilmore, the author of *In Cold Pursuit*, explains that the nasal passages have been cleared of the offending material, say dust or pollen, so the need to expel it more dramatically has been nullified.

It's hard to measure how fast the droplets fly out, but photographic studies of these awesome bodily functions record average distances of five feet. Still, that's no guarantee that sneezing on or near someone you don't like will make them sick. Gilmore says almost all of the droplets broadcast in a sneeze are from the mouth, and that's not where the cold viruses congregate. They stay in the cells of the nasal passages, where they multiply. For this reason, sneezes don't usually carry an infectious dose of cold virus unless the sneeze is done uncovered and with the mouth shut.

And, by the way, if you've been avoiding sneezing because you heard some crazy rumour that it's comparable to dying — relax and let it go. There's no hard science to back up this superstition. What's more, stifling sneezes can lead to musculoskeletal injuries such as slipped discs. Besides, a hefty sneeze, complete with kaboom delivery, can be a healthy thing. If you experience difficulty bringing on sneezes, try external stimuli like looking into bright sunlight, sniffing pepper, or using an electric toothbrush.

Sheetfaced

Adjective:

having lines on one's face made by pillows and sheets.

Submitted simultaneously by Ron Boyle,
Carleton Place, Ontario, and Paul Sullivan, Victoria

It's one thing to sleep like a rock, but quite another to wake up looking like one. Too often, we peer into the mirror wondering if someone has been playing tic-tac-toe on our face all night. The hardest thing is getting rid of these Rip Van Wrinkles. Beauticians say that pulling and pinching our faces only encourages wrinkles. Try rubbing ice cubes on your face in between bites of toast and sips of coffee. Not a great way to start the day, but it's better than turning up at the office **sheetfaced**.

Here are some other clever suggestions from the listeners:

- **cotslot** — Chris Maguire, North Vancouver
- **crevident** — Gio Robson and Paula Migliardi, Winnipeg
- **dreamseam** — Pamela Bond and Shannon Hogan, Toronto
- **drool gutter** — Sabrine Barakat, Richmond, British Columbia
- **percalation** — Vanessa Jacobs, Oakville, Ontario
- **pillowpinch** — Roya Shababi
- **Rip Van Wrinkle** — Bill Plewes, Fraserville, Ontario
- **rumplesheetskin** — Philly Markowitz, host of CBC's *Roots and Wings*
- **scrunchling** — Maurice de Groot, Victoria
- **slimple** — Elaine Simmonds

FYI

Wondering if there are any precautions you can take to reduce the likelihood of getting **sheetfaced**? Well, unfortunately, only millionaires can afford them. The lightness of pure silk sheets might help reduce dreamseams, but they cost as much as $1,200 per sheet or $200 per pillowcase. More durable Egyptian cotton sheets with a thread count of six hundred go for $400 each. Plebs may catch their Z's on percale sheets with thread counts as low as

150, the linen equivalent of burlap, which makes for spectacular **sheetface**. The best strategy for avoiding Rip Van Wrinkles is to sleep on your back.

Slined

Verb:

to get stuck in the slowest lineup in a store or at a bank.

Submitted by Don Spence, Edmonton

The worst thing about waiting in line is that there is absolutely nothing to do. Bored senseless, your mind goes south while your body essentially functions as a bookmark, keeping your place in the never-ending conveyor belt of consumer goods and services. According to the experts, we spend approximately half an hour a day in lineups. Businesses know this makes customers angry, but they cling to the human-resources practice of hiring too few clerks for too few dollars. At least in supermarkets you get to read the tabloids for free if the lineup is long enough.

The words suggested by listeners for this annoying fact of life were spectacular. For most, a mighty verb like **slined** did the job, but others preferred the clout of a noun (i.e., "Sorry I took so long with the groceries, honey. I was in queuewait"). Here's the short list:

- **faux-queued** — Edward Murphy
- **line loser** — Marcia Stacy, Sidney, British Columbia
- **linear letdown** — Claire Budziak, Ontario
- **misalined** — Terry and Peggy West, Ottawa
- **misqueue** — Horace Wilkens, Foleyet, Ontario
- **queuebotched** — Beverly Goodwin, Kingston, Ontario
- **queueburn** — Thea Miller, Vancouver
- **queuebyboob** — Nancy Van Patten, Saltspring Island, British Columbia
- **queuewai**t — Melissa Mills, Victoria
- **squeued** — Phil Densham, Barrie, Ontario
- **stagnaqueued** — Kathryn Buck, Toronto

"You get in the fast lane — eight items or less — with ten litres of spring water gripped in one hand and a piglet-sized pouch of slippery 2% under the opposite arm, at the end of which dangles five pounds of potatoes," writes Nancy Van Patten of Saltspring Island. "All the shoppers next to you in the 'slow lanes' are clipping along. They're paying the cashier, bagging the goods, leaving. You, my dear chaps, have chosen the boobyqueue. And you look like, you feel like, and you are a queuebyboob."

FYI

While a source of frustration for most, lineups are a source of endless fascination for others. Dalhousie University industrial engineering professor John Blake is an expert in applying queuing theory to real-life situations, like lineups in hospitals. He found that the waiting period in emergency rooms could be reduced if staff came on duty two hours before the busiest times to prevent a backlog. He also suggested having a fast-track line for runny-nosed kids and others who aren't there for anything serious. Here's hoping somebody in charge of health care reads his study soon and decides to apply some of this revolutionary common sense.

More jargon from the fascinating world of lineup science:

- **bulk arrival:** a whack of people arriving somewhere at the same time.
- **reneging:** when people get so frustrated that they leave a lineup and go home.
- **balking:** what people do when they see a long lineup and decide not to line up at all.
- **recycling queues, retrial queues:** joining a lineup, deciding it's too long, leaving, then coming back later.

Slipsdream

Noun:

the dream that cannot be remembered; not an interrupted
dream so much as a dream that resists capture.

Submitted by G. R. Clayden, Fredericton

Remembering a dream in the morning can be like trying to hold on to sand under water — as you try to remember it, or recount it to a bedmate, the dream fades away.

The **slipsdream** certainly does slip away, just beyond our reach. Perhaps it gets driven back by the current of air generated by the blinking of your eyes as you wake up.

Here's the short list of other listener suggestions:

- **dream cleaver** — Elizabeth Kwiecien, Bedford, Nova Scotia
- **dream leaver** — Tom Mitchell, Port Perry, Ontario
- **dream puffs** — Karl Pfeifer, Saskatoon
- **dream snatcher** — Darlene Boudreau, Beresford, New Brunswick
- **dreamclipse** — Sue Gillespie, Peace River, Alberta
- **dreamnesia** — Bonnie Dawe, Thrumstone Landing, Ontario
- **dreamslip** — Kathleen Williams, Georgetown, Ontario
- **ephemerêve** — Karen Harding, Richmond Hill, Ontario
- **evaporêve** — Nola Keeler, Whitehorse, Yukon
- **fleet dreams** — John Olivier, Milton, Ontario

- **Freudian blips** — Murray Hiebert, Calgary
- **liminal letdown** — Cathy Wills, Lansdowne, Ontario
- **morning thickness** — Ken Turner
- **nightzheimers** — Jerome Gagnier, Georgetown, Ontario

FYI

Ask a Freudian why we forget our dreams, and he'll say something about repression and an unconscious unwillingness to deal with the darker, submerged self. Ask a New Ager, and you'll be told it's because you are too stressed out and surface from the psychic depths too quickly. On a more logical note, the "salience hypothesis" contends that some dreams are more memorable than others owing to their emotional impact — we remember pleasant and hopeful dreams because they represent a life we wish for. Similarly, we recall nightmares because their content is so horrendous.

Undercarment

Noun:

the coattail, dress hem, or seat belt that hangs out the door of moving vehicles.

Submitted by Mallory Burton

It's no fun wearing salt- and grease-stained clothing after you've dragged it through miles of mud and slush on your way into the office. But try signalling to another driver that she's dragging an **undercarment** and you're likely to get another kind of hand signal. Oblivious, she drives on. Maybe she's conducting road tests for Ralph Lauren — how many miles of pavement does it take to shred a raincoat?

Here's the short list of wonderful listener suggestions:

- **autodangler** — Roy Olynick, West St. Paul, Manitoba
- **carbage** — Sharen Malone, Cranbrook, British Columbia
- **carbungle** — Jon Percy, Granville Ferry, Nova Scotia
- **carnacle** — Peter Spearey, Brandon, Manitoba
- **cartail** — Christopher Redd, Winnipeg
- **carticle** — Joanne Dionne, Englehart, Ontario
- **door danglies** — Chris Lambie, Halifax
- **doorjam** — Mark Mazerolle, Winnipeg
- **doornamentals** — Brian Martin, Kitchener, Ontario
- **doorphan** — Mary Monteith, Kitchener, Ontario
- **draggle** — Wes, Mississauga, Ontario
- **drag-strip** — Charlie Kyte, Dunsford, Ontario
- **dud flap** — Doreen MacLean, Vancouver
- **flapsam** — Eugene Mlynczyk, Bradford, Ontario
- **road mop** — Philip and Marie Garrison, Saint-Polycarpe, Quebec
- **slam gunk** — Doug Millman, Burk's Falls, Ontario
- **strapdragon** — Kris Kiviaho, Elliot Lake, Ontario

Undercarment

With all the clever ways drivers carry things on the outside of their cars, it's a wonder why anyone bothers to put any goods inside. Listeners sent in some very entertaining stories about the **undercarments** they have witnessed or instigated. It does raise the thorny question of whether we can call something sitting on the car roof or bumper an *under*carment . . . Maybe "carnacle" is a better all-purpose word for that.

"This summer, while travelling on the Bicentennial Highway just outside Halifax, I approached a car that was dragging behind it six or eight feet of rubber gas-pump hose. The hose was still attached to the gas-pump nozzle, which in turn was firmly lodged in the gas-tank door on the rear passenger side of the vehicle. I stayed behind the car for less than a minute, as I took the next exit, but was left wondering, given the noise and commotion the event would have caused at the pumps, how much longer it would be before the driver would become aware of the situation."

— *Keith MacInnes, Victoria Mines, Nova Scotia*

Megan Reekie of Ottawa wrote that she recalls seeing "the former mayor of Ottawa, Jacqueline Holzman, leaving the official chain of office on top of her car at an event in 1996 while her driver just peeled away."

Kathleen Ryan says she's heard about a lady in Sudbury who drove to Lively, Ontario, at ninety kilometres an hour with a dozen eggs clinging to her bumper! "All arrived safely and breakfast went off without a hitch."

Adam Rudzki of Sault Ste. Marie, Ontario, writes:
"While working in Chapleau (in the mid-1970s), I stopped
at a local restaurant to pick up a pizza for supper. I drove all
the way home, and only when I was parking in my driveway
did the pizza slide down from the roof onto my hood."

Alexander A. MacIntosh of Kentville, Nova Scotia, writes:
"I had a delightful view of a friend of mine driving away in
his Volvo sans toupée. A closer inspection revealed said
toupée clinging for dear life to the driver's door."

Eugene Mlynczyk of Bradford, Ontario, says he remembers
seeing "a string of linked sausages being dragged from the
rear of a station wagon" when he was a young boy.

Anita McWilliams of Hudson's Hope, British Columbia,
says she drove around with an axe on the top of her Subaru
wagon for two weeks. The axe had become wedged between
the rack and the car roof. "Occasionally I would hear a
clunking sound and would glance in the rear-view mirror,
thinking maybe I had dropped the muffler, but nothing
untoward appeared on the road. By the time I got home,
I had forgotten about it. Two weeks later, I happened to
approach the car from the passenger side and finally saw the
axe blade hooked around one of the roof-rack supports."

One of a Kind

Our search for Wanted Words turned up some unexpected windfalls. Listeners occasionally sent in — unbidden — their own fully formed words, which, far from being AWOL, are doing active duty in the field. In most cases, listeners made up these words themselves. At other times, the linguistic lineage was unknown, but the word has proven so useful they've grafted it onto their vocabulary wholesale.

Some of these words are provided here. Spread them around liberally — after all, you can't copyright a word, and who knows, they may just end up in *The Oxford English Dictionary* some day.

ambisinistrous *(adjective)*:
equally inept with both hands; opposite of ambidextrous.
Mike Tucker, Toronto

amblivious *(adjective)*:
uncertain and oblivious (i.e., don't know, don't care).
Elizabeth Howard, Bella Coola, British Columbia

blade runner *(noun)*:
the small strip of grass the lawnmower cannot reach.
Joanna Crilly, Kars, Ontario

blamestorming *(noun)*:
when co-workers or managers sit in a group and discuss
why a deadline was missed or a project failed and whose
fault it was. Colin Cliveson, Edmonton

blotion *(noun)*:
the opposite of suction. Jeff Challoner

booterhooters *(adverb)*:
a term describing the planned or accidental occurrence of
two or more people matching in some way (i.e., by wearing
the same thing). "Mother had sailor suits for all the boys and
would dress them up booterhooters every chance she got."
Coined by the eight-year-old sister of Brigid Lynch,
Combermere, Ontario

brinkle *(verb)*:
when bright, twinkling rays of light reflect on water, they
are brinkling. Hilary Vavasour, St. John's

catterel *(noun)*:
what you get when you put doggerel to equally appalling
music. Edith Robillard, Latchford, Ontario

chype *(verb)*:

correspond in a chatty manner, as is frequently seen in e-mails. "I was chyping to Paul the other day . . ." Riisa Walden, London, Ontario

compucate *(verb)*:

(of a computer) make simple tasks unnecessarily complicated. "Things got compucated when I tried to buy a pack of gum at the store. It took five employees, huddled around the computerized cash register, ten minutes to take my eighty-five cents." Christopher Menu, Edmonton

crapitalism *(noun)*:

an economic system that derives wealth from seducing people into consuming vast amounts of crap, including appliances that break easily, useless toys, plastic everything, junk food, etc. Gary Boyd, Montreal

drismal *(adjective)*:

Hank Dayton in Waterloo uses this word to describe "those dismal, drizzly November days when the damp and chill penetrate you to the very marrow and only the thought of single malt Scotch gives you the strength to go on."

dronker pipe *(noun)*:

the corrugated metal drainpipes used in ditches and culverts. Kevin Sheldrick, the son of Patricia and Douglas Sheldrick of Brantford, Ontario, came up with this word at age eight.

ehsayer *(noun)*:
slang term for a Canadian. David Medd, London, Ontario

elbonics *(noun)*:
what two people do on trains, planes, or in theatres when they fight for the armrest. Anonymous

frasorial *(adjective)*:
referring to a set of non-identical twins of which one is male and one female. Moyda Silver, Toronto

fringers *(noun)*:
very cold fingers; commonly associated with winter. Paula and Anne Marie Hendry, Beaverton, Ontario

infanticipation *(noun)*:
the state of anticipation parents experience during pregnancy. M. Rankel, Edmonton

gherkinectomy *(noun)*:
the removal of a pickle from a pickle jar with a sharp utensil. Dorothea Helms, Sunderland, Ontario

gleep *(verb)*:
to smile vacuously during posed photographs. "Aunt Rosa insisted that we all gleep into the camera, even though the meal was charred and inedible." Warren McBurney

hurg *(verb)*:
hug someone so hard it almost hurts. Allyson Mitchell, Toronto

lapkin *(noun)*:

Sheila Fairley of Toronto says her neighbour's child coined this clever improvement on the word "napkin."

newscake *(noun)*:

attractive young newsreaders and reporters who land jobs on TV much more frequently than their older, homelier peers. David Robinson, Toronto

nolf *(adjective)*:

lacking the ability to perceive smells. "The Who has a new theme album about a teenage girl who is nolf." Leon Surette, London, Ontario

nuff *(verb)*:

what cats do when they rub up against a person or furniture. "The cat was nuffing my leg." Marilyn Lerner, Toronto

paramates *(noun)*:

two people who live together romantically but are not married (a.k.a. co-vivants). Norma West Linder, Sarnia, Ontario

runchy *(adjective)*:

describing the pushed-in face of a pug dog. The five-year-old daughter of Carol Kruse of Victoria, British Columbia, made up this word when she first saw a pug dog, later adding, "His face is all runched up" and "He's a little runcher."

sleeperistic *(adjective)*:

inducing sleepiness in a person. Pauline Watkin

slounge *(verb)*:
flake out, relax, and do nothing. "I slounged the day away reading trashy magazines and watching the soaps." Serena Rykert, Lake St. Peter, Ontario

snards *(noun)*:
the muddy ice clumps that form behind car wheels in the winter. Charlie Kolompar, Rexdale, Ontario

starter marriage *(noun)*:
a short-lived first marriage that ends in divorce with no kids, no property, and no regrets. Also, starter wife, starter husband. Lyndon Sharp, Saskatoon

stouff *(noun)*:
a shrub wrapped in burlap for the winter. "The stouff on Fred's front lawn looks like a person waving for help." Shannon Purves-Smith

tastualize *(verb)*:
the ability to conceptualize what something will taste like based only on a list of ingredients. "I'm tastualizing ginger, garlic, sesame, and portobello mushrooms on crispy rice — mmmm, delicious." Pauline Weber, Oakville, Ontario

testeria *(noun)*:
the male equivalent of hysteria; antisocial behaviour believed to derive from the gonads. Virginia Buchanan-Smith, Cambridge, Ontario

thunder-sponge *(noun)*:
someone who constantly attempts to spoil a story or humorous anecdote by stealing the punchline or diverting the spotlight to himself. Gordon Ogenski, Trail, British Columbia

ultimatyum *(noun)*:
the last morsel left on a plate, saved for the last bite.
"Is that an ultimatyum on your plate, or should I put it in the dog bowl?" Robert Bott, Calgary (Larry Rapshaw of Oswego, New York, calls it a delectabit)

unlax *(verb)*:
unwind and relax simultaneously. Jennifer Lunergan, Fredericton

wonderstanding *(noun)*:
the feeling of enlightenment and joy you experience upon finally seeing and understanding something you've only read about in books. Jeff Gottfred, Calgary

yardening *(noun)*:
what a person does with a rake and wheelbarrow in his yard.
"I do more yardening in the fall when the leaves turn."
George Proctor, Keewatin, Ontario

We're always interested in hearing your suggestions for other lingusitic gaps that need to be filled. You can write to us at:

> **"Wanted Words"**
> c/o This Morning
> CBC Radio One
> P.O. Box 500, Station A
> Toronto, Ontario
> M5W 1E6

Our e-mail address is wantedwords@cbc.ca. And you can follow our contest by visiting our Web site: Go to www.cbc.ca, look for the links to radio program sites, click on *This Morning*, and you'll see our Wanted Words icon. We look forward to hearing from you!